Starting with
story

Fairy tale activities
for early years

Pauline Kenyon

Author
Pauline Kenyon

Editor
Jane Bishop

Assistant editor
Sally Gray

Series designer
Joy White

Designer
Anna Oliwa

Illustrations
Louise Gardner

Cover
Sarah Laver

Designed using Aldus Pagemaker
Processed by Scholastic Ltd, Leamington Spa

Published by Scholastic Ltd, Villiers House, Clarendon Avenue,
Leamington Spa, Warwickshire CV32 5PR

© 1997 Scholastic Ltd Text © 1997 Irene Yates
2 3 4 5 6 7 8 9   7 8 9 0 1 2 3 4 5 6

British Library Cataloguing-in-Publication Data
A catalogue record for this book is available from the British Library.

ISBN 0-590-53655-9

Contents

chapter four

Cinderella

chapter five

Little Red Riding Hood

Fairy stories must surely rank amongst some of the most fascinating tales ever told. They are full of magic, adventure, fantasy and the ultimate triumph of good over evil. Most of them have origins going back hundreds of years, indeed many of the stories we enjoy and think of as being part of our own tradition and history were often first told in very different cultures and countries. For example, a Chinese version of Cinderella can be traced back to 850 AD!

The tales seem timeless, being originally told by word of mouth from one generation to the next, retaining their general storylines but adding a richness in the different details and interpretations added by each storyteller. Today technology brings new dimensions through animations and spectacular pantomime and theatrical productions. These stories form part of the literary heritage of our children, and they are always fresh to each new group who encounters them, joining the ranks of countless generations of small children who have listened in wonder and delight.

Learning potential

In many homes however, the regular reading and sharing of fairy stories is less common than in the past. Such stories – if familiar to children at all – are often limited to video versions which are sometimes viewed in isolation from the rest of the family. However, most early years' practitioners, in a wide variety of pre-school and main school settings, read and enjoy using traditional fairy stories with young children. They know

very well that children's imagination will be stimulated by the exciting adventures and that they will respond with pleasure. Often, the full learning potential of the tales is not fully exploited.

Desirable Outcomes

This book uses five well-known fairy stories as starting points for further learning. The five stories – Jack and the Beanstalk, Snow White and the Seven Dwarfs, Sleeping Beauty, Cinderella and Red Riding Hood – have been used as a framework for activities to promote learning in all areas of the National Curriculum and also religious education. These activities also support the *Desirable Outcomes for Children's Learning* for five-year-olds identified by the School Curriculum and Assessment Authority. In this way the book provides an appropriate curriculum for playgroups, pre-school groups and nurseries, as well as contributing to the curriculum for children in school reception classes.

Each chapter provides two activities each for English and mathematics, one each for science, geography, history, art, music, PE and RE and two for design and technology to include one cookery activity and one 'design and make' task. The *Desirable Outcomes for Children's Learning* link to these subjects with English as Language and Literacy; mathematics remaining the same; science, technology (including cookery), history and geography coming under the heading of Knowledge and Understanding of the World; PE encompassing Physical Development which incorporates fine motor skills in a

range of other subjects; art, music, drama and dance contributing to Creative Development and RE supporting spiritual development. Many of the suggested activities also strongly reinforce Personal and Social Development.

Practical activities

The book has been designed to suit the needs of early years' practitioners. The chapters can be followed through in sequence or activities can be chosen randomly to provide a rich and varied range of practical tasks. You may wish to select one particular story which has specific appeal, as each chapter has been constructed to be free-standing and used independently. The whole programme can be covered from beginning to end or dipped into over a longer period of time, or revisited from year to year, without direct repetition. This should be useful for those settings with mixed-aged children who need to devise a form of rolling programme in their planning.

Each page contains a new activity which is laid out in the same format each time to help busy staff prepare materials and quickly ascertain what needs to be done in preparation for the session. Special discussion points are highlighted in order to reinforce the learning objectives and there are suggestions for support and extension work for both younger and older children which should be particularly helpful for staff working with mixed-age groups. In addition, there are a range of follow-up activities listed to develop the learning programme even further, and many of these suggest links with parents, visitors and the wider community.

Cookery

Establish a regular hygiene routine before any cookery activity, making sure all children wear a protective apron and wash their hands thoroughly. Be sensitive to individual children's cultural or religious customs, and practices such as vegetarianism which will limit the consumption of some foods. Ensure that you are aware of any food allergies, intolerances or special dietary requirements and that all relevant information is documented for other staff.

Extension activities

In each chapter, two display activities are outlined which are designed to enrich the learning environment and also to extend young children's experiences. At the end of the book a section of photocopiable sheets provides two sheets to accompany each chapter and these form the basis of at least two of the activities. Often the illustrations provided on these pages will prove useful as they can be copied and enlarged for display purposes or in other work you are undertaking with your children.

Although it is not essential to cover each activity in any chapter, following the whole schedule will give a well-balanced programme of practical and imaginative activities, covering all areas of the curriculum. This should enable young children to explore a wide range of appropriate, stimulating and enjoyable activities which are related to the magical world of well-loved fairy stories. What better way can they be introduced to the richness of this literary heritage and further their learning in so many vital areas?

chapter one
▶ **introduction** ◀

Jack and the Beanstalk

Jack and the Beanstalk, is often performed in pantomime and the tale is told in a variety of ways in children's books. The simple story has magic running through every section and children relate with delight to the different parts of this traditional story. There are many versions available, but the activities in this chapter are based on this Victorian story.

═══════

Jack and his widowed mother are very poor. They live in a tiny cottage and when their cow cannot give milk any more, Jack's mother tells him to sell the cow at the market so they have some money to buy food.

On the way to market Jack meets a man who offers to give him five magic beans for the cow. Jack is happy to do this and runs back home with the beans. His mother is very cross with Jack because they need money not beans! She is so angry that she throws the beans out of the window and sends Jack to bed without having his tea.

Next morning Jack and his mother are amazed to see that the beans have grown into the most enormous beanstalk. It has a stem as thick as a tree, stretching high into the clouds above their heads. Jack begins to climb the huge beanstalk, fighting his way between the huge leaves. Right at the top he finds a winding road leading up to a gleaming castle, towering above him. He arrives at the castle and in the gigantic kitchen he meets a giant woman.

Jack is very hungry and he asks her for some food. She kindly gives him an enormous bowl of porridge, but before he can eat anything the ground shakes and a thunderous voice echoes round. The woman tells Jack to hide before her husband the giant arrives crying:
'Fee–fi–fo–fum, I smell the blood of an Englishman,
Be he alive, or be he dead, I'll grind his bones to make my bread!'

The giant doesn't find anyone and so he eats his dinner. His magic harp sings soothing music whilst his magic hen lays golden eggs. After eating his dinner he falls asleep. Jack grabs the magic hen and runs away, but the harp makes a noise and the giant chases after Jack.

Jack quickly climbs down the beanstalk and when he gets to the bottom he uses his axe to hack down the beanstalk. The giant is following Jack down the beanstalk and he falls to his death when Jack cuts it down.

So Jack and his mother have the hen which lays the golden eggs and all the money they need and live together happily ever after – thanks to the five magic beans!

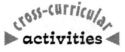
What comes next?

Objective
English – to develop sequencing skills.

Group size
Small groups or whole class.

What you need
Sheets of A4 card, copies of photocopiable page 87 (enlarged to A3 size), four sheets of A2 sugar paper, string, Blu-Tack, adhesive, broad felt-tipped pen.

Preparation
Make an enlarged copy of page 87 (to A3 size), cut out and mount the illustrations onto card. Fold the sheets of sugar paper in half and run string around the fold, tie it firmly keeping a hanging loop at the top.

What to do
Explain that you are going to make a group book to tell the story of Jack and the Beanstalk. Tell the children to listen very carefully while you tell the story because they will need to remember the order in which things happened in the story.

Tell the story or read it aloud and then show the children the cards you have prepared. Explain that some of the pictures for the book are jumbled up and will need sorting out into the right order. Hold up the picture of Jack and his mother and tell them that this starts the story. Put it on the floor or Blu-Tack it to a wall or the board. In turn, hold up each card and ask the children to decide where it comes in the story, leaving spaces in which to fix the other cards. Encourage them to explain their reasons for the order of the pictures, using words such as 'before' and 'after'.

When the sequence is correct, glue the cards into the 'book' – one per page. Hold the book up and ask the children what you should write as a caption under each picture.

Discussion
When telling the story ask the children: what happened before Jack did this? Why did this happen? What do you think will happen next? When holding up the cards say: did this happen at the beginning of the story, in the middle or near the end? Check with the children if they think the cards are in the right order.

For younger children
Break the story down into chapters and restrict the activity to only a few cards. Write the children's words in the 'book' before moving on to the next chapters. Retell the story a little at a time.

For older children
Ask a small group of children if they can work together and sort the cards themselves and then explain to you how the story develops. Let them glue the cards into the 'book' and write their storyline ideas on paper before choosing which ones they will write into the 'book'.

Follow-up activities
▲ Paint illustrations for the book cover.
▲ Use computers to write text for the book in different large fonts.
▲ Learn the 'Fee-fi-fo-fum' chant and recite it walking like giants.

cross-curricular ▶ activities ◀

Spot the difference

Objective
English – to develop visual discrimination and memory and to extend vocabulary.

Group size
Up to six.

What you need
A large tray containing: two large leaves, two gold-painted hard-boiled eggs, a large 'giant's' boot (adult walking boot), five beans, foil covered chocolate coins and a feather. A small table cloth, a shopping bag and a scarf.

Preparation
Cover the tray containing the items with the table cloth.

What to do
Ask the children to guess what's under the cloth. Accept all the guesses, however unusual but ask them to consider if the thing they suggest would really fit on the tray. One-by-one reveal each item and remind the children where it figured in the story. Tell the children to try and remember all the items on the tray.

Next, cover the tray up again and explain that you are going to remove one item. Ask the children to close their eyes, and carefully slide one of the items into the shopping bag. Uncover the tray and ask if they can see what's missing. When they have made some guesses show which item you had removed.

Let the children take turns being blindfolded with a scarf while another child removes items from the tray to hide in the bag. Remove the blindfold and see if the child can identify what's missing. When they have guessed let them check in the shopping bag. Give all the children a turn at guessing and choosing if possible.

Discussion
Encourage the children by taking a turn at guessing yourself and pretending you can't solve the problem. Say that you will need them to help and ask: is it big or small? What colour is it? Who does it belong to?

For younger children
Start with only three items on the tray such as the feather, the boot and the eggs. Pass the objects around the group and let the children have a close look. Remove the items yourself and let the children feel in the bag to guess. Build up the number of items when you think the children are ready.

For older children
Write the names of the items on card and place the card labels by the items themselves. Play the game with the name labels rather than the items, starting with three, reading them together and building up the number used as the children become more proficient.

Follow-up activities
▲ Hide one of the objects in the room and ask the children to find it, playing 'hot' and 'cold', giving 'getting warmer' directions as the children search.
▲ Place a tiny ribbon on some dolls or teddies for the children to spot.
▲ Lay the table in the home corner and leave out one item. Can the children see what's missing?

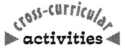
Three golden eggs

Objective
Mathematics – to aid one-to-one counting skills.

Group size
Small groups or pairs.

What you need
Two large dice, yellow and brown counters, cards with the numbers 1–12 written in numerals and words, a small container for each child's egg counters (jar lids, saucers or egg cups).

Preparation
Make the cards with large, clear numerals and words underneath. Make two large dice from cube shaped boxes or large wooden bricks. Cover each side with a numeral (1–6, 7–12) and pictures of the same number of golden eggs.

What to do
Give each child 12 counters to represent their 'golden eggs' and tell them to put them in their own container. Next let each child in turn roll the dice and count the score they get. Hold out the cards and ask the child to match it to the right number card.

Hand the card to the child and ask them to count out the right number of their 'golden egg' counters in front of it. If they are right, they keep the card, if wrong it goes back in the pack. Put the counters back in the container to use on the child's next turn. Continue until all the cards are won – the child with the most is the winner!

Discussion
Ensure that each child counts the numbers out loud and the others listen carefully to check that it's correct. Ask them to count again when they are matching the eggs to the card, so that the idea of one-to-one correspondence – each counter is counted against each egg picture – is developed. As the game develops, stop and count how many cards each child has won.

For younger children
Only use one dice numbered 1–6 and give younger children more help with the counting activities and in taking turns with the dice.

For older children
Use a dice with only numerals and words, no pictures. Ask them to make up their own matching games.

Follow-up activities
▲ Decorate hard-boiled eggs with patterns using brushes and yellow vegetable colouring. Decorate blown eggs with gold felt-tipped pens or paint and hang on a small branch stuck into a flower pot.
▲ Find out how real hens live.
▲ Make a collection of hard-boiled hens' eggs and sort them by size and colour (link with 'The magic sandwiches' on page 22).
▲ Read the story of *Chicken–Licken* (Traditional).
▲ Make simple egg–cosies out of felt.

▲ **10**
Starting with story
Fairy tale activities

The giant's castle

Objective
Mathematics – to increase awareness of different shapes.

Group size
Small groups or working individually.

What you need
Photocopiable page 88 – 'Build a castle', colouring pencils or crayons, scissors, glue and spreaders, sugar paper.

What to do
Hand out a copy of the photocopiable sheet to each child and ask them to colour in the shapes using crayons or colouring pencils. Encourage them to colour as neatly as they can and to stay within the lines. When they have finished, they can cut out the shapes and stick them on to a sheet of sugar paper to make a castle shape.

Discussion
Look around your room and identify things which have the same shape such as square floor tiles, rectangular windows or circular plates. As they work, ask them to tell you the correct names, and to count how many of each shape they have. Ask: how many blue triangles have you made? How many small squares have you got? When their castles are finished, ask them to say how many of each shape they used – write this on the bottom of their picture.

For younger children
They will need help cutting out the shapes, or you might decide to pre-cut them.

For older children
Working in pairs or small groups the children can combine all their shapes and make a larger castle. Ask them to draw some extra shapes to make a giant, copying the original shapes carefully and keeping a tally of how many of each shape they use. See who can use the most shapes in their pictures, the most triangles or the most squares. Can they put an S on every square, an R on every rectangle and a C for each circle – or even write the whole word on the biggest shapes?

Follow-up activities
▲ Make a collection of objects of different shapes, cut out from catalogues and magazines.
▲ Use sticky coloured shapes to make pictures relating to the 'Jack and the Beanstalk' story.
▲ Paint big shapes on the playground or hall floor and play 'follow my leader' naming the shapes.
▲ Play 'I Spy a square shape beginning with....'

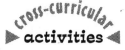
The magic beans

Objective
Science – to look at how seeds grow.

Group size
Small groups or the whole class.

What you need
A jam jar for each child, packets of mung beans, alfalfa or other sprouting beans, squares of cotton big enough to cover the jar top, elastic bands, jug of water, sticky labels and pencils.

Preparation
Prepare a clean jam jar, elastic band and cotton square for each child. Have a jug of water ready. Read the instructions on the seeds – most seeds will be ready for eating after about five days or so. You will need to time the 'planting' activity carefully to ensure the crop is ready on a convenient day – especially to link in with 'The magic sandwiches' on page 22.

What to do
Ask each child to pour in enough seeds to cover the base of their jar and add sufficient water just to cover them. Put the cotton cover over the top and secure it with an elastic band. Write the children's names on the sticky labels and fix them to the jars. Put the jars on a window ledge or similar position. Each day tip the jars upside down to let the old water out through the cloth and add a little fresh water – just enough to cover the seedlings – and gently shake the bean sprouts. When they are about 3 cms long and ready to eat, rinse them and use them in sandwiches or in salads.

Discussion
Show the children the packets of seeds and explain that they are going to grow their own bean sprouts to eat. Read the instructions and ask: how long does it say these beans will take to grow? Are they all the same or different? How? Encourage talking about the process of planting and watering – Are the beans floating? What will happen to the beans? Why do they need water? Each day, ask the children to look and smell carefully and to describe any changes in the beans. Warn them that not all seeds are safe to eat.

For younger children
You will need to help younger children by pouring the water and fastening the bands. Have their names written ready on the labels.

For older children
Let them write their own name labels. Ask them to keep a growth diary each day by drawing a sketch of their beans and the changes they can see. You could help them write a short sentence under each entry.

Follow-up activities
▲ Let a few bean sprouts grow really long and then plant them into pots.
▲ Cook a simple stir-fry of bean sprouts, add soy sauce and let the children taste some Chinese style cookery.
▲ Plant other vegetable seeds – marrows, peas, beetroot.

The castle and the cottage

Objective
Design and Technology – to make buildings from reclaimed materials.

Group size
Small groups or whole class.

What you need
Illustrations of castles and houses (from magazines), a collection of boxes of different sizes (some large and some small), cardboard tubes, card and different coloured papers, scissors, sticky tape, PVA adhesive, thick paint in a range of colours, paint brushes, pencils and paper, aprons.

Preparation
Prepare illustrations or collect pictures of castles and small houses or cottages. Arrange the materials in piles ready for the children to sort through.

What to do
Remind the children that Jack and his mother lived in a tiny cottage because they were poor and that the giant lived in a very large castle because he was so big and wealthy. Tell the children that they can choose to build either Jack's cottage or the giant's castle.

Show them the pictures which you have gathered and point out the different features. Ask them to use these pictures to give them ideas for their own constructions. Let them explore all the materials available and then build their models. Leave the models to dry if necessary and the children can then paint them.

Discussion
Ask the children to choose which building they want to make and then ask them about the boxes and materials they will need to use. Draw attention to the differences in size and the suitability of the junk materials they choose. Ask: will that be big enough for the giant's castle? How big will your model be? How big would Jack's cottage be then? Try to extend their vocabulary – Do you think the castle will have towers? Will it have a draw-bridge? Encourage them to think about their model – how will you get the windows to open? Where is the giant's kitchen? How will you make Jack's garden? What colour is best for the roof? Why?

For younger children
They will need help with choosing their materials and cutting and fixing the pieces together.

For older children
Ask them to look at the available materials and draw a simple diagram plan of how their model will look. Ask them to make some moving parts such as doors which will open.

Follow-up activities
▲ Ask the children to explain to each other where the different parts of the story happen in their models.
▲ Go for a walk around the neighbourhood looking at different buildings and deciding what they are used for – shops, houses, offices, doctors' surgeries and so on.
▲ Build different sized houses out of LEGO or construction kits.

The giant's kitchen

Objective
History – to find out that things change over time.

Group size
Small groups.

What you need
A collection of kitchen artefacts and pictures of kitchens (old and new), sheets torn from mail order catalogues or kitchen brochures, large and small sheets of paper, pencils, scissors, glue and spreaders.

Preparation
Label the large sheets of paper, one with 'The giant's old kitchen' and the other with 'New kitchens' and lay both sheets on the floor.

What to do
Show the children the pictures and artefacts which you have collected from modern kitchens and talk together about the things found in kitchens nowadays. Encourage the children to share their knowledge with you.

Now remind them of the story and that this happened a long time ago. Show them the artefacts and pictures of older kitchens.

Finally ask the children to consider each picture or object as you hold it up and to decide which is the appropriate sheet 'Old' or 'New'. Ask the children to cut out pictures, or draw pictures of old and new kitchen artefacts and stick them on the sheets.

Discussion
Ask the children to look carefully at the objects and try and name them and say what they are used for. Explain what kitchens used to be like and how gadgets have changed, for example look at an old whisk compared with a newer electric mixer; a fire grate oven compared with gas/electric/ microwave cookers; flat iron with an electric iron. Highlight the changes in materials – such as the use of plastics for modern items.

For younger children
Concentrate on cutting and sticking things found in a modern kitchen. Provide larger pictures and help with the cutting out.

For older children
Encourage them to work together to choose pictures of different objects so that only one of a type goes into the new kitchen and similarly, draw and stick their ideas for the Giant's old kitchen.

Follow-up activities
▲ Look at and classify other old and new things such as toys and clothes.
▲ Visit a local museum or heritage property.
▲ Invite an elderly person to come and talk about their childhood memories and how things have changed.

The view from the beanstalk

Objective
Geography – to find out how views change depending on how high up you are.

Group size
Small groups or whole class.

What you need
A camera (Polaroid if possible), pencils and paper, a large sheet of paper with a beanstalk drawn along one side, a climbing frame or similar safe apparatus.

Preparation
Explore the local environment to pinpoint places where children will be able to see different views, for example from the upstairs floor of a building, on higher ground or from apparatus. Arrange for access and organise any extra helpers which you will need. Make a collection of photographs taken from a high viewpoint, such as aerial photographs or postcard views.

What to do
Tell the children that they are going to think about how the view that Jack could see changed as he climbed up the beanstalk. Explain that they are going to draw the view that they can see from different heights. Let them have a look around and talk about what they can see.

Next, take the children to visit the places at different heights which you have already identified. Can they tell you what different things they can see because they are higher up? Take a photograph of the view with the children watching you.

Back at your base ask the children to draw what they saw from the different places. Cut out their pictures and stick them alongside the beanstalk. Add the photographs which you have taken when they are available.

Discussion
It is important for the children to realise that they will have a different view depending on where they are. Ask them to imagine they are Jack and ask them: what would Jack see now? What's different at this height? What do the houses/ people/cars look like now? Show them the photographs to show how things look from increasingly high altitudes.

For younger children
Restrict the heights: start by letting them lie on the floor to see what they can see and then do the same standing up. Later they can look out from an upstairs window or, with adult support, from a climbing frame.

For older children
Ask them to draw their own beanstalk showing all the things Jack could see from the top.

Follow-up activities
▲ Make a large map or plan of the immediate area, let the children each draw their own houses and stick them in the correct place.
▲ Make a height measuring-chart on the door like a beanstalk and mark in everyone's height on the correct leaf.
▲ Go for a walk outside and look to see what an ant might see, what a cat or a dog might see and what a bird might see at their different heights.
▲ Talk about the order of height of different buildings in the area.

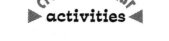

Jack's journey

Objective
Art – to make leaf prints.

Group size
Small groups.

What you need
A collection of different large flat leaves or large cut out leaf shapes, thick mixed paint in several different shades of green, sheets of foam larger than the leaves, plastic plates or containers to hold the foam, large brushes, large sheets of paper.

Preparation
Place the foam sheets on the plates or containers. Tip the paint on to the foam and work the colour well into it by twisting it or by using a large brush.

What to do
Tell the children that they are going to make a beanstalk out of leaf prints. Show them the different leaves and talk about the shapes. Demonstrate by pressing each leaf into the foam and then transferring it to paper, pressing it down firmly. Carefully remove the leaf to reveal the print.

When they are ready to try, let each child print several different leaves in different shades of green and leave them to dry. Later cut them out and stick them in pairs on to a display area to make the beanstalk.

Discussion
Talk about the different leaf shapes, extending vocabulary by identifying veins and stalks. Ask the children to look at the different shades of green and see if they can match the colours to the real leaves. Ask which colours are lighter and which are darker. Ask them to say what other things they can think of which are shades of green.

For younger children
Help them with the process of pressing into the foam and applying even pressure to the print. Use two very different shades of green to reinforce the difference, working up to more subtle differences.

For older children
Invite them to print their leaves in pairs ready for the display. Ask them to make other regular patterns with their leaf prints.

Follow-up activities
▲ Count and number the leaves up to ten.
▲ Print the leaf patterns onto plain fabric using fabric paints to make curtains for the play house, floor cushions or storage bags.
▲ Paint a large block of each shade of green and make a collection of objects to match.

▲ 16
Starting with story
Fairy tale activities

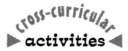

Up and down the beanstalk

Objective
Music – to become aware of loudness and softness and higher and lower notes (dynamics and pitch).

Group size
Small groups or whole class.

What you need
Range of instruments – bells, tambourines, clappers/castanets, maracas, drums, and other untuned percussion instruments – these can be home-made shakers, drums and blocks. Tuned percussion instruments such as chime bars, glockenspiel or xylophone, and different beaters. A cassette recorder.

Preparation
Collect the range of instruments together and choose a quiet spot for the activity. Set up the cassette recorder.

What to do
Tell the children that they are going to compose special music to sound like the magic beans growing and Jack and the Giant on the Beanstalk. Hold up each untuned percussion instrument in turn and show them how it can be played.

Distribute the instruments and ask them each to play their instruments softly like the beans beginning to grow, getting louder as the beanstalk grows. Ask a child to 'conduct' the music from when it starts, as it gets louder until it stops.

Then demonstrate the tuned instruments, showing how the notes can get higher or lower. Let the children take turns to play bean-growing music. Ring the changes with Jack's climbing music, Jack's flight down and the Giant's fall. Let them practise and then tape their composition. Then play it back to them!

Discussion
Ask: how can we make gentle/loud music? Ask them to tell you how their instrument makes its sound and talk about the different types of sound they make. With the tuned instruments, ask them to decide which are high and low notes.

For younger children
Concentrate on getting them to start and finish together, watching for the signal to play softly and loudly.

For older children
Let them work in pairs to compose their own growing or climbing music, performing it to the other children.

Follow-up activities
▲ Play musical 'follow my leader' copying the loudness or softness of the leader.
▲ Make musical instrument shakers out of washing-up liquid bottles, filling them with dried peas, seeds, sand, salt or small buttons.
▲ Classify instruments according to whether they are blown, beaten, shaken, plucked or bowed.

Up we grow!

Objective
PE – to develop body control and spatial awareness.

Group size
Whole class.

What you need
Cassette tapes of recorded music, a glockenspiel or xylophone and beaters, large empty space for free movement.

Preparation
Either make tapes of the children's own growing and climbing/descending music (see 'Up and down the beanstalk' page 17) or tape other suitable music.

What to do
Tell the children they are going to make up a dance in which they will 'grow' just like the magic beanstalk. Ask them to each find a space and to listen carefully to the music you are going to play.

Play the instrument slowly, working from the lower to the higher notes. Ask the children to start by imagining that they are the magic beans asleep in their seed cases, and that they 'grow' very slowly in time with the music. Repeat the exercise several times, varying the speed of the music, and adding growing and shrinking. Invite the children to demonstrate their dances to the other children.

Next ask the children to listen to the cassette tapes and to make up their own growing dance in time with the music.

Discussion
Talk about how seeds grow and ask the children how they could show this in their dance. Ask them to choose which part of their bodies will grow up first, last, the highest. Will they grow up straight or twirl round? Encourage the children to contribute their own suggestions and demonstrate their ideas.

For younger children
Let them imagine their beanstalk can move around, twisting and turning as it goes, then sinking slowly down again.

For older children
Allow older children to work in pairs to make up a growing dance together, or let some children play the music for the other children to dance to.

Follow-up activities
▲ Move to music which sounds like Jack climbing the beanstalk, Giants moving, magic hens and harps.
▲ Learn some activity rhymes such as 'The farmer's in his den'.

The giant's treasure

Objective
RE – to reflect on things which are precious to different people.

Group size
Whole class.

What you need
A collection of things brought from home which are precious to you and the children. Ensure there is a range including photographs, souvenirs, clothes, objects, books and toys. A safe space to display them, card, felt-tipped pens.

Preparation
Ask the children and adult helpers to bring in things which are precious to them and display them in a safe place. Make a large title 'Things that are precious to us'. Cut and fold cards ready for labelling each item.

What to do
Remind the children of the story of Jack taking the cow to market and getting the magic beans, the giant's precious hen with the golden eggs and the magic harp to soothe him.

Show the children the range of things which you have in your collection – including some ordinary, inexpensive things which are precious to you and explain why these items are special. Ask other helpers to do the same.

Encourage the children to show their precious things and to say why they are special to them. Write a label for each one saying 'This is precious to… (name) because (reason)'.

Discussion
Explain to the children that everyone has some things which they think are precious.

Sometimes these are valuable, sometimes they are just special. Invite the children to show their precious thing and ask them: who gave it to you? When did you get it? Is it old or new? Why is it precious to you? Where do you keep it? How would you feel if you lost it? Discuss how we should look after other people's precious things properly. Ask them if Jack was really right to steal the giant's precious things!

For younger children
Help younger children to answer the questions, give them possible suggestions to choose from if necessary.

For older children
Let older children make a book called 'Our precious things' in which they can draw illustrations of their special belongings with some words to support the pictures.

Follow-up activities
▲ Read *Dogger* by Shirley Hughes (Red Fox).
▲ Do a survey of things that are precious to parents and grandparents.
▲ Make a treasure chest from an old cardboard box and make necklaces and bracelets from 'beads' made from scrunched up foil and sweet wrappers.

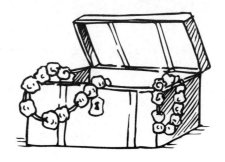

▲ 19
Starting with story
Fairy tale activities

The magic beanstalk

Group size
Small groups.

What you need
A length of rope, green crêpe paper, large green cut out leaves, white paper, backing paper, boxes and cylinders (foil inners), thick white and yellow paints, brushes, Sellotape.

Preparation
Wrap the green crêpe paper around the rope and fasten it. Fasten the leaves in pairs at intervals along the rope. Paint numbers on the leaves. These can be used for counting activities. Cover the display area with white backing paper to represent

clouds towards the top of the board. Fasten the beanstalk so that it appears to disappear into the clouds at the top and grows from the ground at the bottom. Draw in some distant mountains, some nearer hills and rivers, forests and other interesting features.

What to do
Ask the children to each draw small houses and tiny people (this can be linked to 'The view from the beanstalk', page 15) and arrange these around the bottom of the beanstalk. Help the children to fasten the boxes and cylinders together to make a three-dimensional castle shape and then let them paint them with the thick paints to make the giant's castle. When this is dry, fasten it on to the clouds.

Use the display as an aid to counting – ask the children to count the leaves as you point to them and also say how many pairs of leaves there are, ask them to look carefully and count how many people and houses there are on the display.

Discussion
Ask the children to count the leaves together as you point at them from bottom to top. Older children can also count down from ten to zero, like a rocket launch, to get used to counting up and down. As the children choose shapes for the castle ask them: what part will this be? What does the giant do there? Which is the way in? Where does the hen live? Point to the different height leaves on the beanstalk and ask: what would Jack see from here? Could he see over the houses? Could he see the hills? Could he see the castle yet? Stress that at higher viewpoints he would be able to see more.

In the illustration: What can Jack see from leaves 1 and 2? What can he see from the other leaves?

Follow-up activities
▲ Make a display of what an ant might see in the grass.
▲ Collect photographs and pictures of tall and short buildings.
▲ Find out about life in a place too far away for you to see.

The giant and Jack

Group size
Small groups.

What you need
Several large sheets of sugar paper fastened together (big enough for an adult and a small child to lie on and be drawn around), pencils, paints, paper, brushes, scissors, adhesive, backing paper, large paper labels, felt-tipped pens.

Preparation
Cover the display area with backing paper. Draw round a tall adult wearing trousers lying on the large sheet of paper to form the rough shape of the giant. Draw over the outline and draw in giant style clothes. Draw round the smallest child and complete this figure of 'little Jack'.

What to do
Encourage the children to help you complete the scene by painting in the details. Draw around life-size plates, cutlery, mugs, shoes, hats, pillows and other everyday objects.

Make a corresponding set drawing around doll-sized equivalents. Fasten the giant to one side of the board, surrounded by all the giant-sized paraphernalia, and Jack to the other with all the doll-sized equipment. Put a selection of large and small sized objects in the middle and ask the children to identify who they belong to. Add some labels naming the owners of the different items.

Discussion
Ask the children to look at the two figures and say what they look like. Introduce words like big, huge, enormous and little, tiny, small. Point to the different sized objects and ask the children to say to whom it belongs and why.

Follow-up activities
▲ Read *The great big enormous turnip* by Alexei Tolstoy (Heinemann).
▲ Make hats, aprons, bibs or belts for dolls and teddies of different sizes. Use comparative language to describe them.

The magic sandwiches

Group size
Small groups.

What you need
Brown and white thin sliced loaves, six hard-boiled eggs, bean sprouts (either grown from the activity on page 12 or bought from the supermarket), salt, pepper, mayonnaise, soft butter or spread, plates, basins, spoons, forks, spreading knives, a sharp cutting knife, serving tray or platter.

Preparation
Hard boil and cool the eggs. Carefully wash and clean the bean sprouts and put them in a small bowl. Arrange the ingredients and equipment on a table. Make sure the children wash their hands thoroughly.

What to do
Explain that the children are going to make 'magic sandwiches' with golden eggs and bean sprouts. Demonstrate how to shell an egg and then let the children take turns to try. Put the eggs into a small bowl and use a knife to chop them finely. Help the children to add a little salt and pepper and two to three teaspoonfuls of mayonnaise.

Next, ask the children to butter some brown and white bread and let them spread a little of the egg mixture on a white slice of bread, cover it with bean sprouts and top it with a brown slice. Carefully cut the sandwich into quarters and let the children arrange them on the serving plate. Serve and enjoy the food!

Discussion
Explain that the egg has changed because it is hard-boiled, talk about other ways that eggs can be cooked. Look at the shells and talk about the different colours. Ask the children what it feels like shelling the egg, what does the contrasting texture of the shell and egg feel like? Ask the children to count out the spoonfuls of mayonnaise together and let them say what it feels like stirring the mixture. Talk about spreading the butter on to the bread – count the sides and corners, what

shape is the bread? Talk about safety in using sharp knives and introduce the words 'halves' and 'quarters' as you cut the bread and they count the pieces. Count all the sandwiches to see if there are enough for everybody. Discuss correct manners in serving and being served.

Follow-up activities
▲ Have a teddy bears' tea party with a range of other sandwiches.
▲ Make or decorate invitation cards and invite parents or helpers to tea.
▲ Make decorated place-mats and party hats.

chapter two
▶ introduction ◀

Snow White and the Seven Dwarfs

The exciting story of Snow White offers a wealth of opportunities to explore themes of contrasts – different times, places, moods and characters, families, types of vehicles, even sizes and kinds of apple! Snow White provides many opportunities to extend language and mathematical experience and to explore issues in the world around us. The activities in this chapter are based on the following version of this well-loved story.

When Snow White was born her mother, the young queen died. The king remarried and his new wife was the most beautiful but most vain woman in all his kingdom. Every day she would stand in front of her magic mirror and ask: 'Mirror, mirror on the wall, Who is the fairest one of all?' and the mirror would reply: 'Queen, you are the fairest one of all!' Time passed and Snow White grew into a lovely young woman. When the proud queen asked the mirror her usual question she was horrified to hear: 'Queen, you were the fairest, it is true. But now Snow White is more beautiful than you!'

The queen was very jealous of Snow White and she plotted to kill her. She ordered her huntsman to take Snow White into the woods and kill her, bringing back her heart. The huntsman knew that murder was wrong, so he took Snow White into the deepest woods and left her there taking back the heart of a deer.

Snow White wandered into the forest until she found a tiny cottage and went inside. Upstairs she found seven little beds and she was so tired that she lay down to sleep. Later, seven dwarfs returned home from their work mining gold in the mountains and discovered her! They agreed that she could stay with them and they warned her to take care and not let any visitors into the cottage. For they knew that the evil queen would find out she was alive and would come looking for her.

The dwarfs were right. One day the queen dressed as an old woman pedlar, came to the cottage and sold Snow White a magic comb which poisoned her head. The dwarfs found her unconscious, but they managed to save her.

The queen tried again, she came to the cottage disguised as a farmer's wife and gave Snow White a poisoned apple. This time the dwarfs were too late to save her life.

Snow White was put into a glass coffin. A prince found the coffin and entranced by her beauty, he lifted the lid, the apple fell from her lips and she woke up. The couple fell in love and were married. When the evil queen heard the news she was so angry that she fell down dead and Snow White lived happily ever after.

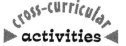

Who are the dwarfs?

Objective
English – to extend vocabulary.

Group size
Small group or whole class.

What you need
Seven pieces of A3 card, scissors, felt-tipped pen, 21 pieces of card, string, fabric and paper in seven different colours, glue and spreaders. Photocopiable page 89.

Preparation
Enlarge photocopiable page 89 seven times and cut and stick each dwarf on to a sheet of A3 card. Draw on seven different faces/characteristics. Sort fabric and paper into seven colours and cut into pieces about 1 cm square, place them in a container. Prepare glue and spreaders.

What to do
Tell the children that no one knows what the names of the seven dwarfs really were and that you are going to name them yourselves. Ask the children to suggest names, discuss them and select seven which can then be written on card.

Now ask the children to look at the pictures of the dwarfs and to suggest some describing words for each dwarf. Select two suggestions for each and write these on some pieces of card. Finally, let the children work together to dress a dwarf, sticking on squares of fabric in only one colour. When the decoration is complete, ask the children to find the correct name and describing words for each dwarf and to attach these to his picture. Now suspend the dwarfs in a display.

Discussion
Ask the children to look at the pictures for clues which might make them think of a name. Ask: do you think he is happy or sad; clever or silly; sleepy or wide-awake? Is he thin or tubby; neat or scruffy? Ask them to explain their answers to you. Can they suggest words to describe those features? Help by suggesting some to them or remind them of words in the story.

For younger children
Give them help sticking and making the collage. Retell the story emphasising words which might help them choose characteristics later.

For older children
Ask them to make their collage to show the character of their dwarf, for example, untidy clothes, choosing a colour that suits their name – such as red for an angry dwarf.

Follow-up activities
▲ Make up a class story about the dwarfs before Snow White came to stay.
▲ Turn the home corner into the seven dwarfs' cottage.
▲ Make simple puppets of the main characters in the story.

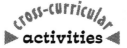
The magic mirror

Objective
English – to stimulate imaginative ideas.

Group size
Small groups or whole class.

What you need
Photocopies of mirror sheet for each child, (see 'Preparation') plus one for demonstration, pencils, felt-tipped pens, crayons, scissors, adhesive, a collection of magazines, a large mirror.

Preparation
Draw a simple oval mirror shape onto an A4 piece of paper. Leave plenty of space inside the mirror for the children's drawings. Photocopy this for each child and have the other materials ready.

What to do
Show the children a real mirror and invite individual children to have a look in it and to say what they can see! Then angle the mirror slightly and ask them to describe what they can see in it now. Let several children have a turn.

Next, show the children the mirror shape on the photocopied page. Tell them that this is their magic mirror and they can choose to add their favourite things as a reflection. Demonstrate on your own copy of the mirror and draw in the shapes of your own favourite things – animals, food or people – to give them ideas.

Using the magazines let the children cut out pictures to stick on the mirror shape or they can draw their own ideas directly on to the shape. When the pictures are complete, write the relevant word under each choice.

Discussion
Talk about the things you have chosen and explain why you want them in your magic mirror. Explain that because the mirror is magic the children can choose anything at all to put in their reflection. When they finish, ask each child to hold their mirror up and to say what they have chosen. Ask them why each thing is special – is it because they have one at home? Is it the colour, taste, smell? How big are they? Why have they chosen the people or animals? What are their names? Where do they live?

For younger children
Help younger children to choose and cut out their pictures, or let them draw just one or two special things.

For older children
Let older children cut, stick and draw independently and they can then copy the sentence 'In my magic mirror I can see.....' underneath. Some children will need help to write in the names of the objects.

Follow-up activities
▲ Let the children bring in their favourite things for a collection with labels.
▲ Learn the wicked queen's chant 'Mirror, mirror on the wall' and act out being the wicked queen.
▲ Ask the children to find out about other uses of mirrors (such as wing mirrors in cars, dental mirrors and kaleidoscopes) and ask if they have seen 'magic mirrors' (at fairgrounds) which distort images.

Seven dwarfs

Objective
Mathematics – to match and sort correctly.

Group size
Small groups.

What you need
Photocopiable page 90 and a pencil for each child, crayons or felt-tipped pens – in seven different colours.

Preparation
Copy the sheet in advance.

What to do
Hand out a photocopied page to each child and show them that they have to match the clothes on the washing line to the right dwarf. Ask them to look at the pattern on each dwarfs' trousers and then find his hat, socks and scarf to match.

Tell the children to join up the right clothes to the correct dwarf with a pencil line. They can then colour in each dwarf and his matching clothes so that all seven dwarfs are in a different colour.

Discussion
Ask the children to look very carefully at the different clothes and the patterns. Are they plain, spotted, striped, checked? How does the pattern go – across, downwards,

diagonally? Is it dark or light? Point to each garment they choose and ask them to check that it matches. Then ask them what colours they will choose, remind them that each dwarf must be different to the others. Only have seven colours available to avoid confusion.

For younger children
Enlarge the sheet to A3 size and cut out the items. Let the children sort them into groups, colour them and stick them on paper.

For older children
Invite them to count the number of hats, socks and scarves and let them complete the sentence that you write: 'There are ... dwarfs and there are ... hats, ... scarves but there are ... socks!'

Follow-up activities
▲ Match different coloured socks in pairs and count in twos.
▲ Dress teddies or dolls in different clothes for different occasions.
▲ Wash the dolls' clothes and hang them out to dry, counting all the garments.

Apple fun

Objective
Mathematics – to sort and classify by size and colour.

Group size
Small groups.

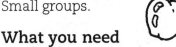

What you need
A collection of apples – different sizes (cooking apples, eating apples and windfalls) and different colours. Three large sheets of paper, green and red felt-tipped pens.

Preparation
Gather together a collection of different sized and coloured apples. Label the sheets: 'Red apples', 'Green apples' and 'Red and green apples' using the appropriate coloured felt-tipped pens.

What to do
Tell the children that you have some apples for them to sort into different groups. Ask them to look at all the types and sizes of apple you have but to concentrate on the colour first.

Put the labelled sheets of paper out and read aloud the labels you have written on them. Now pick up an apple and ask the children to decide which sheet it should go on. Read the words out again and then put the selected apple in the right place. After a few practice runs let the children take turns to pick an apple and place it on the relevant sheet. When they have sorted by colour ask the children to put each group of apples into order of size starting with the biggest first.

Discussion
Ask the children to look carefully at each apple. Ask: is it green, red, or green and red? Read the labels for the children but ask them to try and read them out loud, point out which letter sound the words begin with and ask them to say the phonic sound. For the size activity, pick up two apples and ask: which is the biggest? Then compare it with other apples: is this bigger than that one? Continue to ask some comparative questions to help the children decide. Are they all getting smaller now? Is the first one really the biggest? Which is the smallest?

For younger children
Restrict the number of apples and make the differences in size and colour very obvious.

For older children
Ask them to count the apples in each group and write the total number on the sheets. They can then write a separate number for each of the apples in their group, placing the biggest apple on number 1 and so on.

Follow-up activities
▲ Cut the apples into halves and show that two halves make a whole one.
▲ Try the different apples for a snack and vote for the juiciest.
▲ Plant apple pips and see if you can grow an apple tree.

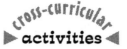

Shiny reflections

Objective
Science – to develop observational skills and to look at reflective surfaces.

Group size
Small group or whole class.

What you need
A collection of shiny objects such as: spoons, saucepans and kitchen equipment, mirror and foil; non-reflective objects and some which are partially reflective such as mugs, shiny book covers, smooth-surfaced plastic items. Three hoops or trays to contain the items, card, felt-tipped pens.

Preparation
Use the card to make three labels: 'Reflects a lot'; 'Reflects a little' and 'Does not reflect', to correspond to each hoop/tray.

What to do
Tell the children that you are going to sort the things into groups according to how they reflect light. Place the hoops on the floor and read the labels aloud explaining the words carefully. Hold up the mirror and ask the children which hoop/tray it goes in. Then take turns for each child to select an object and put it into the correct place.

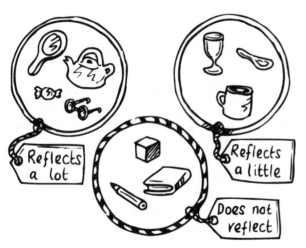

Discussion
Ask the children if they can see themselves, or anything else, in the surface of the objects. Do their reflections look the same in the other things as they do in the mirror? Help

them observe the distortions caused by curved surfaces and the reversed image on the inside of a spoon. Ask each time: does it reflect a lot, a little, or not at all? Why do you think this happens?

For younger children
With younger children, just use two hoops and ask them to try and decide whether the item is shiny or dull. Are they able to identify things in your room or setting that are also shiny or dull?

For older children
Give them three labelled sheets of paper and ask the children to draw the different reflective, partially reflective and non-reflective objects on to the correct sheet. Can they think of any more objects to include?

Follow-up activities
▲ Go for a walk and look at large reflective surfaces in the environment.
▲ Cut out collections of reflective surfaces from magazines and catalogues.
▲ Make a collage using reflective foil, sweet wrappers and shiny bottle tops.

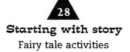

Dwarfs at work

Objective
Design and Technology – to make a model with moving wheels.

Group size
Small groups.

What you need
Some large boxes, paper plates, paper-fasteners, thick paints and brushes, string and card.

Preparation
Make sure you have four plates for each box and sufficient paper-fasteners. Remove any sharp staples in the boxes.

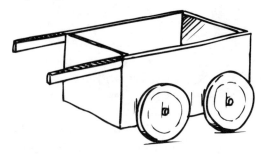

What to do
Explain that you are going to make trucks for the seven dwarfs to put their mined gold in. Point out that they will need wheels to make them move and a handle or some means of pulling them along. Let the children work in pairs to design their trucks, showing you where the wheels and pulling device will go. When they have decided on their construction you can fix them in place (paper-fasteners are too difficult for small fingers, and holes need making for string).

The models can be completed by the children painting them carefully with thick paint to cover up any wording on the boxes.

Discussion
Ask the children to talk through their ideas before they begin. Encourage pairs to decide together what they will do. Ask: where do you want the wheels? How will the dwarfs pull it along? What colours will it be? Why? Which dwarf will it belong to? When the models are made encourage the children to explain to each other how they made them.

For younger children
Give help positioning the wheels and handle.

For older children
See if they can think of any different ways of making wheels which will go round. Let them explore construction kits for ideas for their box model.

Follow-up activities
▲ Learn to sing 'Heigh Ho, Heigh Ho it's off to work we go!'.
▲ Make gold nuggets from play dough, painted clay or Plasticine.
▲ Invent a 'going to work, mining the gold and coming home' dance.
▲ Make a large truck from a robust construction kit and test its strength with a heavy load.

▲ 29
Starting with story
Fairy tale activities

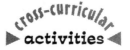

When did it happen?

Objective
History – to sequence events on a simple timeline.

Group size
Small group or whole class.

What you need
A collection of photographs or pictures of babies, toddlers, young and old people, a large sheet of paper (A2 size,) felt-tipped pens and Blu-Tack.

Preparation
Rule the sheet into three columns, labelled 'A long time ago'; 'Some time ago' and 'Not long ago'.

What to do
Tell the children that some things in the story of 'Snow White' happened a long time ago, when Snow White was only just born, whereas other things in the story happen when she is much older. Retell the story asking the children to say how old Snow White might have been when events happened and pointing out how everyone changes as they grow older and time passes.

Next, tell the children that you are going to sort some pictures of people you have collected into the times when they were born. Show the children the columns and read the titles. Then show the pictures one at a time and discuss which is the most likely column for each one to go in and place it correctly. When the sorting is complete, focus on the similarities of people in the same columns.

Discussion
Ask the children to say which events happened first, later on and last in the story. Ask: how old would Snow White have been when she was a baby/sent out with the huntsman/grew up in the dwarfs' cottage/was tricked by the evil queen/

married the prince? Stress the passing of time and how some things happened a longer time ago than others.

Ask the children to look carefully at the pictures for clues. Is the person old, young, or in the middle? How can you tell? Ask them about their own families: who is the oldest/youngest? Time is a difficult concept for young children so be prepared to explain about older and younger, using families as examples.

For younger children
Divide the sheet into 'Old' and 'Young'.

For older children
Have a number line from 0–70, divided into tens, and help the children put the pictures on the timeline guessing approximately how old the people might be.

Follow-up activities
▲ Sort pictures of old and new houses, everyday things, cars, toys and so on.
▲ Make a week timeline to show when different things happen such as television programmes or nursery/school events.
▲ Start a weekly class diary.

Different places

Objective
Geography – to learn about the features of different locations.

Group size
Small groups.

What you need
A collection of different sized and shaped boxes and containers, tubes, other reclaimed materials, card, adhesive, scissors, pebbles, sand, lolly sticks, used matchsticks, twigs, Plasticine, straw or raffia, thick paint, palettes and brushes. Cardboard for model bases. Pictures of castles, cottages, woods and mountains as inspiration.

Preparation
Sort the materials into groups of things that would be useful to make a castle, a cottage, woods, and a goldmine entrance.

What to do
Tell the children that there are many different places in the Snow White story. Ask them to remember the evil queen's castle, the forest and the dwarfs' cottage. Talk about the differences in surroundings (such as the goldmine in the mountains). Tell them that they are going to make the different places so that you can compare them.

Divide the children into groups or pairs and give them the materials for specific models, such as twigs and Plasticine to make the forest and let them look at the pictures you have available. Make the models and use them to talk about similarities and differences in locations.

Discussion
Look at the pictures together and ask: what would a castle be like? Is it larger or smaller than a cottage? What would it be built of? What might a cottage be made of? Also ask: what would live in a forest? Where does the gold come from? How do they get into the mountain to dig? When the models are complete, ask: what is the same about a castle and a cottage? What is different? Is it the same in a forest as underground in a mountain?

For younger children
Give them more information about castles, cottages and goldmines before they start modelling.

For older children
Help them label their models such as 'mine entrance', 'deepest forest', 'Queen's room'.

Follow-up activities
▲ Look at large scale local maps and identify houses, shops, the school and other features.
▲ Look at photographs of very different places (deserts, islands, hot and cold lands) and talk about the differences.
▲ Go for a walk in the locality and notice the different locations.

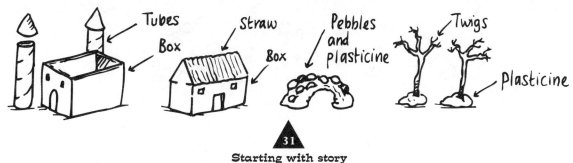
Tubes · Straw · Pebbles and plasticine · Twigs · Box · Box · Plasticine

Mirror, mirror on the wall

Objective
Art – to make close observational drawings.

Group size
Small group or whole class.

What you need
Paper and a mirror for each child (ensure that these are safely framed or with taped edges), drawing pencils, felt-tipped pens, chalks, pastels or other mark-making tools, a reproduction of a self-portrait – such as Van Gogh.

What to do
Show the children the self-portrait and explain that lots of artists draw and paint themselves, especially in the days before cameras were invented, and that they use mirrors to help them see the details. Use any examples you have to discuss the way the artist has made the self-portrait. Now ask the children to look in their mirrors and describe their own images. Draw their attention to the shape, size and position of the different features.

Explain that the children are now going to try a self-portrait of their own. Let them choose different drawing tools and try to make a drawing of themselves. Make sure they constantly use the mirror for reference. Compare the results drawn in different media.

Discussion
Explain that in the time of Snow White, with no cameras, the only pictures would have been painted by artists. Looking at the self-portraits you have, ask: how has this artist made this picture? What ways has he/she made marks – are they thick, thin, straight, wavy or a mixture? Discuss the shape of the face. How far up do the eyes come? This is generally about half way down the face. When the children are looking in the mirrors, ask: what is the shape of your face? Are the eyes drawn in the right place? Is the nose the right size compared with the eyes? When completed, ask each child to describe the portrait.

For younger children
Give them help by looking with them at their reflection and pointing out features and positions.

For older children
Let them compare self-portraits by different artists from different periods.

Follow-up activities
▲ Look at how artists have represented other people in portraits.
▲ Collect photographs of the children and compare their colouring, skin tone, facial shape and hair styles. (Be sensitive to individual children.)
▲ Look at illustrations in books and magazines and how people are depicted.

Dwarf music

Objective
Music – to explore sounds made by different instruments.

Group size
Small groups of 11 or whole class.

What you need
A range of instruments – drums, triangles, shakers, chime bars, tambourines, and bells for example.

Preparation
Ensure there are at least eleven different instruments or range of beaters so they can be played differently.

What to do
Explain that the children are going to compose a sound story for Snow White.

Demonstrate how to play the instruments, and let the children listen. Draw their attention to the differences in sound and differences which a hard or soft beater makes. Ask them to choose instruments to represent Snow White, the evil queen, the huntsman, the seven dwarfs and the prince.

Retell the story and 'conduct' the musicians in when their character is mentioned. Ask them to play to show the mood – for example emphasise the angry evil queen, the sad dwarfs and the happy, charming prince.

Discussion
Ask the children why they have chosen their instrument. What kind of sound does it make? How many ways can you play it? Can you play it loudly/softly/slowly/quickly?

For younger children
Help younger children to choose their instruments, or use some simple home-made shakers or drums.

For older children
Ask them to work as a group to compose their own section of the story, such as the discovery of the dwarfs' house or the wedding scene.

Follow-up activities
▲ Tape the composition and use it for dance or drama work.
▲ Listen to music showing different moods (sad/joyful/soothing/discordant).
▲ Invite the children to make up words for a Snow White song to a familiar tune such as 'London's Burning' or 'Ring of Roses'.

Heigh ho!

Objective
PE – to move in a variety of ways individually and in groups.

Group size
Large groups or whole class.

What you need
A large space (indoors or out), a cassette recorder and tape of music made up of different moods – from page 33 or a pre-recorded mixture of slow, fast, sad, happy pieces with very different styles.

Preparation
Format the tape with short sections (one or two minutes each) of contrasting music.

What to do
Talk about the work the seven dwarfs had to do – digging and scraping for gold in the mine, pulling heavy trucks along, sorting the gold, marching to and from work, doing the chores and gardening for example. Ask the children to demonstrate appropriate movements for each action. Rehearse them and improve them.

Play the music and ask the children which movements fit best to the different sections. Let them move to the music, practise their dances and perform them to each other.

Discussion
Let the children describe their actions. Ask: which parts of your body are you using? Do you need to make big or little movements to show digging? How would you move if you are pulling a really heavy load? Let individuals or small groups perform and ask the others: what did they show us?

For younger children
Let them work as individuals, or pairs, on only one or two different movements such as digging for gold and pulling the trucks.

For older children
Ask them to work in small groups and make up a sequence of movements, changing from one action to a very different one, to fit in with the changes in the music.

Follow-up activities
▲ Play 'Follow my leader' copying the leader's changing movements.
▲ Have team relay races passing a baton moving the fastest and then the slowest ways possible.
▲ Act out a day in the life of the dwarfs.

Family life

Objective
RE – to examine the way people live in different families.

Group size
Small groups.

What you need
Magazines and catalogues, pencils, paper, scissors, adhesive, felt-tipped pens, sheets of card.

Preparation
Make zigzag books from the card, entitle one end 'Living in a family'.

What to do
Talk with the children about living in families, explaining that families can comprise many different groupings. Be sensitive to single parent or other family groupings. Discuss things that people do in families and how different it would be living all on your own.

Ask the children to choose some favourite family scenes to draw or paint. Ask them to each supply a picture or a collage showing different scenes of family life and stick them altogether into the class zigzag book. Write an explanatory sentence under each child's picture.

Discussion
Talk about your family, those who live at home and those who visit. Ask the children: how many people live in your house? Who visits sometimes? What do you like doing as a family? Encourage them to talk about their pictures as they design them. Compare sizes of families, count brothers, sisters – and pets!

For younger children
Act as scribe for their sentence, help with cutting out small shapes.

For older children
Let them copy or write their own sentences and glue their own illustrations into the book, or they could make their own individual zigzag books.

Follow-up activities
▲ Make a pictogram of the number of people in everyone's family living at home.
▲ Classify different animal families – birds, insects, reptiles, mammals or things that swim, fly, crawl or walk.

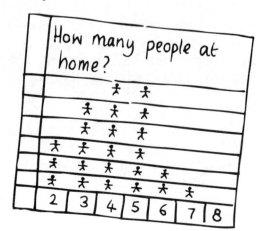

Mirrors on the wall

Prints made from comb →

Mirror made from foil ↓

Children's drawings

Prints from apple halves →

Snow white was very ill

Snow white's wedding day

Group size
Small groups.

What you need
A roll of wide cooking foil, large sheets of cardboard, paper, thick paint, brushes, scissors, PVA adhesive, spreaders, polystyrene trays/plastic containers, sheets of foam, several large apples – cut in half, card for titles, felt-tipped pens.

Preparation
Cut out large oval, circular or square shapes from the cardboard. Smooth foil carefully over the cardboard and fasten securely at the back. Draw large comb shapes on the foam sheets and cut them out. Fill the plastic trays with the thick paint.

What to do
Tell the children that they are going to make mirror pictures to show the Snow White story. Show them the different mirror shapes and ask them to choose which part of the story will be shown in each mirror. Ask them to paint their characters from the story and leave them to dry. Demonstrate how to print the apple shapes by painting the flat surface of the apple with the thick paint and pressing it firmly on to paper. To print the comb design, gently lie the foam shape flat into the tray of paint coating it lightly then press it on to paper. Leave the prints to dry. Cut out the characters and stick them on to the mirror scenes. Then put the mirror shapes on the wall in order, surrounding them with cut out prints to make an attractive edging pattern. Add captions to tell the story.

Discussion
Discuss the details of their pictures with them, ask: how will the queen look? What will the dwarfs wear? What colours will you choose? Give them opportunities to talk to the rest of the group about their illustrations.

Follow-up activities
▲ Mount all the mirrors to make a large class book of the story.
▲ Use the mirrors as 'props' and do a presentation of the story to parents.

Suspended dwarf characters

Group size
Small groups.

What you need
About 14 sheets of A2 card (or packing case cardboard), sticky tape, pencils, scissors, glue, spreaders, fabric scraps in seven different colours, wool scraps, string.

Preparation
Sort the fabric scraps into seven colours and cut them into small pieces. Tape the card together in pairs to make double length sheets.

What to do
Choose seven small children and ask them to lie down on the card sheets. Carefully draw round their bodies to make dwarf shapes. Adjust them where necessary and add a hat. Draw in guidelines for the beard, trousers, belt, waistcoats and boots on both sides of the figures.

Let the children select one colour and stick on shades of just that colour to dress their dwarf, adding beards, glasses and so on to complete the characters. Let the children draw in the facial features. Next cut the whole figures out neatly and complete the collage on the reverse side. Then add a name card (from the off-cuts), put string through a sticky tape reinforced hole and suspend.

Discussion
Encourage the children to select their fabrics carefully by asking: what would look good as a belt? Why have you chosen that fabric for his boots? How many shades of blue can you count? What texture has this fabric got – shiny, dull, rough, smooth? Ask each group to choose a name for their dwarf. When the dwarfs are completed ask the children to talk about

the size order and the differences and similarities in costume, for example, ask: have they all got boots on? Who has the smallest hat?

Follow-up activities
▲ Make other characters from the story in the same way.
▲ Make smaller, individual figures that stand up with a card prop or support.
▲ Ask the children to make puppets from paper bags, decorated with scraps and drawings and act out the story for the rest of the group.

Unpoisoned toffee apples!

Group size
Small groups.

What you need
One small apple and a strong lolly or barbecue kebab stick for each child, a very large saucepan, wooden spoon, small cake cases, 450g (1lb) soft brown sugar, 350g (12 oz) salted butter, 1 teaspoon of malt vinegar, 150ml (5 fluid oz) water.

Preparation
Let the children wash the apples carefully and push a stick firmly into each one.

What to do
Help the children weigh out the ingredients. Make sure that the children are kept safely away from any heat source. Put all the ingredients into the large saucepan and bring them slowly to the boil over a low heat – about 10–15 minutes – stirring occasionally. When the sugar has completely dissolved, increase the heat and let the mixture bubble steadily – without stirring – for about 12 minutes more. Remove it from the heat and put it in a safe place and allow the mixture to cool for about 15 minutes.

Let each child dip their apple in the mixture. Make sure the children are very careful doing this and if you are in any doubt, let them watch as you dip the apples. Drain off excess toffee and put the apples, stick uppermost, into the cases and then into the fridge to set. Any unused toffee can be poured into a lightly oiled tin, to be broken up and eaten once it has set!

Discussion
As you weigh the ingredients, ask the children: how much do you think you'll need – how many spoonfuls, lumps? Later ask: what do you think will happen when we heat the ingredients up? If the children can safely watch the process, invite them to describe the changes as they occur. Count the number of apples, match them to the cases and count them as they are given out.

Follow-up activities
▲ Visit a supermarket or shop and find out what apples/toffee-apples they sell and where the ingredients come from.
▲ Weigh bags with different numbers of apples in them, predicting and testing which are the heaviest. Arrange them in weight order and compare with the number of apples inside.

Sleeping Beauty

The story of Sleeping Beauty is an excellent vehicle for extending children's learning in language, mathematics and science providing the topics of sleeping, hibernation and the passing of time. The tale gives some good opportunities to look at celebrations such as weddings and birthdays and helps young children to gain a wider understanding in RE, geography and technology. There is also a good range of creative activities in music, art and dance which can be developed from the stimulus of this delightful fairy story, based on the work of Charles Perrault.

Once upon a time, there lived a wealthy king and queen who, after many years of longing, had a baby. They arranged a huge feast to celebrate the birth of their daughter and they invited all the fairies to join the party, but they forgot one. The fairies gathered around the baby's crib and one by one, they gave her their gifts – beauty, kindness and other fine qualities. Just before the last fairy was about to speak, the fairy who they had forgotten raged in and cried out in a hideous voice, 'You forgot me – but you won't forget my gift! When you are sixteen you will prick your finger on a spindle and you will drop down dead!' Everyone was shocked but then the twelfth fairy spoke. 'I cannot undo the gift but I can change it. You will not die but only sleep for 100 years.' The king banned all spinning at the castle and gradually everyone forgot about the awful 'gift'.

When the princess was sixteen she explored some towers in the palace and in one room she found an old lady. 'What are you doing?', she asked. 'Spinning wool at my spinning wheel,' said the old lady 'would you like to try?' The princess took the spindle in her hand and instantly pricked her finger. Immediately she fell into a deep sleep, and everyone in the castle – the king and queen, courtiers and servants – all fell into a deep sleep too. Around the palace a huge thorny hedge of roses grew.

Many years passed, and one day a prince came across the overgrown palace. Drawing his sword he hacked at the rose hedge and he entered the castle without a single scratch. He was amazed to see all the people and animals asleep, snoring gently. He explored the castle and, in the highest turret of the palace, he discovered Sleeping Beauty lying asleep. She was so lovely that he gave her a gentle kiss. The bad fairy's spell was broken and Sleeping Beauty opened her eyes and smiled.

All the people awoke and saw the young couple, who had fallen in love. A wedding was arranged – and Sleeping Beauty lived happily ever after!

Welcome Sleeping Beauty!

Objective
English – to make a greetings card.

Group size
Small group or whole class.

What you need
A sheet of A4 card for each child, pencils and felt-tipped pens, tissue paper, foil and other brightly coloured paper scraps, scissors, glue, spreaders, a selection of greetings cards.

Preparation
Fold each sheet of card in half to make a greetings card shape for each child.

What to do
Tell the children that they are going to make a card for Sleeping Beauty to welcome the new baby, like the ones the fairies may have brought her when she was born. Show them the types of greetings cards in your collection and highlight the different designs. Read out and indicate the print of the text and the greetings which senders have written inside the cards.

Give the children their card shapes and let them draw out their own design, then choose appropriate paper scraps to decorate their cards to make each card special and individual. Ask each child to choose a message for their cards and let them write it in and sign the card.

Discussion
Ask the children what the fairies might have chosen for their cards, would fairy cards be different to ordinary cards? How? Show them the collection of cards and encourage them to look very carefully at the pictures, colours and designs. Read out the text and greetings, pointing out the differences between the printed word and the hand-written greeting. Ask them to listen to things that rhyme and those that don't. Talk about the words they would like on their own cards.

For younger children
Act as scribe to write the words they choose for them.

For older children
Ask them to try and write their own words on paper first, help them with correct spelling and then let them copy it out or write it unaided.

Follow-up activities
▲ Write thank you letters for a gift or for a visit.
▲ Make place-names and place-mats for a party in school.
▲ Paint or print wrapping paper for a birthday or wedding present.

▲ 40
Starting with story
Fairy tale activities

Dream alphabet

Objective
English – to develop a knowledge of phonics.

Group size
Small group or whole class.

What you need
An alphabet line, pencils, felt-tipped pens, two sheets of A4 paper per child, an A1 sheet of paper.

Preparation
Rule each A4 sheet into three rows of five to make 15 boxes to give each child 30 boxes with two sheets. Write a letter of the alphabet in 26 of the boxes. Rule and label the large sheet of paper in the same way.

What to do
Tell the children that you are going to think of the favourite things that Sleeping Beauty, the king and queen, courtiers, servants and animals might have been dreaming of as they slept for 100 years. Refer to the class alphabet line and look at some of the items listed against each letter to give the children the idea.

Show the children the large chart and ask them if they have any dream ideas. Be ready to make suggestions yourself or retell parts of the story to refresh their memory. With each suggestion find the appropriate alphabet letter and draw a quick sketch of the item in the box.

Then give the children their sheets and ask them to think of their own ideas, leading the group and working together one letter at a time. Help the children by writing in the name of the object. This activity is best tackled over several days, completing small sections of the alphabet at each session until the whole chart is completed.

Discussion
As each idea is suggested ask the children to listen carefully and to tell you what sound the word begins with. Be prepared to show them the right letter as it is unlikely that children will know all the letter sounds. Ask them: what favourite things do you think Sleeping Beauty would dream of? What might the horses and dogs dream of? If you had been a courtier what would you have liked to have dreamed about? Have some suggestions up your sleeve for X and Z!

For younger children
Give them suggestions from the story and help them find the right letter box. Restrict the sessions to covering only three or four letters at a time.

For older children
Let them complete the boxes of the sounds they know on their own and then help them with the other alphabet sounds and dream ideas.

Follow-up activities
▲ Learn an alphabet song together or try making up a new one.
▲ Put the children's own names on the alphabet line.
▲ Play 'I Spy'.

Bedtime

Objective
Mathematics – to begin to learn about time.

Group size
Small groups.

What you need
Two large clock faces with movable hands, a sheet of paper stamped with two clock faces for each child ,a small sheet of paper for each child (about 5cm by 10 cm), a large sheet of paper, pencils, crayons.

Preparation
Draw out a pictogram graph (see below). Ask the children (or send a note to parents to find out) what time they go to bed and what time they get up.

What to do
Tell the children that Sleeping Beauty slept for 100 years but most people sleep for only a few hours each night and this varies from person to person. Children usually need more sleep to help them grow big and strong.

Show the children the large clock face with the hands at the time set to 7 o'clock and say that this might be bedtime. Show the other clock with the time set for 8 o'clock as waking-up time. Count together the hours of sleep. Ask the children for their bedtimes and waking times and count them together in the same way.

Draw the hands on the clock stamps and write in the hours for each child. Give out the small pieces of paper and ask the children to draw themselves in their bed for the class graph of sleeping times. Let the children stick their bed onto the appropriate column.

Discussion
What time do the children go to bed? Is it light or dark? Who goes to bed first/next/last in your house? Who gets up first? Ask them what sort of clocks they have at home. Look at the graphs and ask the children to count together the number of beds in each column, then ask: how many hours do most/fewest children sleep?

For younger children
Make the graph showing only bedtimes.

For older children
Let them draw in their own clock hands.

Follow-up activities
▲ Make clock faces to show important times of the day and label them.
▲ Learn 'Hickory, Dickory Dock'.
▲ Make a clock collection.

Sleeping Beauty's necklace

Objective
Mathematics – to make repeat patterns and sequences.

Group size
Small groups.

What you need
A collection of blue, green, red and yellow beads (wooden, clay or play dough – see diagram), long laces with knotted ends, ten cards (about 5cm by 30cm), pencil, felt-tipped pens.

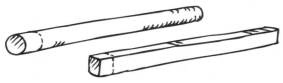

Chop clay shapes

Pierce with a knitting needle and when dry paint in bright colours

Roll out clay or play dough and cut out shapes

Pierce holes. Paint in bright colours

Preparation
Make the beads as shown, prepare the cards to show the beginnings of repeat patterns (drawn using the different bead shapes and colours you have available).

What to do
Tell the children that they are going to finish making pretty necklaces for Sleeping Beauty using the patterns which you have on the cards.

Let them look carefully at the colours and shapes of the beads on the card and they can then thread a necklace of their choice in exactly the same way.

Discussion
Ask them to describe their pattern. What colour bead do you need first? What shape bead must it be? Constantly encourage them to refer to the picture and check their choice against it. When the printed pattern is matched, ask again: now you can see the pattern, which bead do you think you use next? Ask them to look carefully at the sequence of colours and shapes. When it is completed ask them to count the total number of beads and the number of each shape and colour and compare these with other children's necklaces.

For younger children
Only thread by colour pattern.

For older children
Ask them to design and draw their own patterns and make their necklace.

Follow-up activities
▲ Make a collection of different pictures of jewellery and learn the names.
▲ Make play jewellery out of foil, old broken beads and scrap materials.
▲ Set up a treasure chest and 'prince and princess' dressing-up area.

Sleep tight!

Objective
Science – to look at different sleeping patterns and hibernation.

Group size
Small group or whole class.

What you need
A collection of books about animals, including nocturnal animals and those which hibernate, a sheet of A2 paper, Blu-Tack, small pieces of card, tracing paper, pencils, scissors.

Preparation
Trace round and make small labelled pictures on card of a squirrel, cat, dog, hedgehog, mouse, bats, fox, badger, horse, cow, tortoise, lion, elephant, owl, robin or a range of other animals. Divide up the large sheet of paper as shown and pin it on a wall or easel.

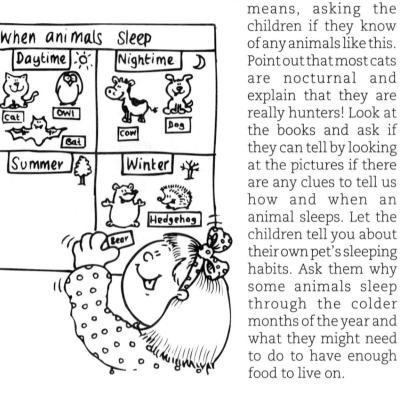

What to do
Explain to the children that although the animals in Sleeping Beauty's palace slept for 100 years, all animals have very different sleeping patterns. Show them pictures of a range of common animals and discuss their sleeping patterns, then talk about more unusual animals. Refer to the books and read sections of text out loud, pointing to the print, and looking at the pictures together.

Take the small picture cards and the larger chart and ask children in turn to fasten the animal where they think it would sleep in the summer and winter.

Discussion
Introduce the words 'nocturnal' and 'hibernate' and explain carefully what each means, asking the children if they know of any animals like this. Point out that most cats are nocturnal and explain that they are really hunters! Look at the books and ask if they can tell by looking at the pictures if there are any clues to tell us how and when an animal sleeps. Let the children tell you about their own pet's sleeping habits. Ask them why some animals sleep through the colder months of the year and what they might need to do to have enough food to live on.

For younger children
Limit the number of animals you learn about to familiar ones.

For older children
Let them draw their own pictures and include the animals.

Follow-up activities
▲ Set up a bird table with bread and peanuts and watch also for squirrels!
▲ Go for a walk in the park and look for signs of wildlife.
▲ Read *Where the Wild Things Are* by Maurice Sendak (Picture Lions).

▲ 44
Starting with story
Fairy tale activities

Magic spinning wheel

Objective
Design and Technology – to construct a model with moving parts.

Group size
Small groups or pairs.

What you need
A selection of construction kits which include wheels, a picture of a spinning wheel, a ball of wool (in a neutral colour).

What to do
Remind the children about the key points of the story connected with the spinning wheel. Talk about the bad fairy's 'gift', about the king banning spinning and the old lady in the turret. Explain how the large wheel turned round and made the spindle spin fast so that the cleaned sheep's wool could be tightly twisted into a thread ready for weaving or knitting.

Show them the wool and untwist a section to shown how it is made up. Ask them to work in pairs or small groups to build a type of magic spinning wheel out of the kits. Let them work together to build their models and then they can explain to the others how it would work.

Discussion
Ask the children: how could you get it to spin round? What would power your magic spinning wheel? What might it be made out of? Which was the part that Sleeping Beauty pricked herself on? When they have built their models, ask them to explain how they want their model to work and encourage the other children to ask questions and make suggestions to further improve their models.

For younger children
Work with large construction kits and help them to fix parts together.

For older children
Let them draw out some of their ideas on to a plan.

Follow-up activities
▲ Learn to weave with paper strips or on a very simple weaving card.
▲ Make a collection of different wheels and things that spin and turn.
▲ Make other kit models that do 'magic' things.

Asleep for 100 years

Objective
History – to recognise old and new objects.

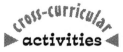

Group size
Small group or whole class.

What you need
Photocopiable page 91, pencils, some new and old artefacts or pictures (toys, clothes, household items, cars, books and houses) red and blue pencils or crayons.

What to do
Explain that things can change a lot in 100 years, so that when Sleeping Beauty woke up some things would look very different to her. Show the children the pictures and artefacts and look at the changes.

Hand out the photocopiable sheet to the children and talk about the pictures together. Ask them to colour in all the new items in red and all the older items in blue.

Discussion
Show the children each picture and artefact and ask them to look very carefully and to guess whether they are old or new. Can they give reasons why? Ask them to look at the materials they are made from, how they are powered and the design. Do they have these now in their houses? Have they seen one like it before? Where? Would Sleeping Beauty have had one in her palace? Explain that we can sometimes see old things in collections and museums.

For younger children
Choose familiar everyday household artefacts to look at and give help with the sheet.

For older children
Let them look at the artefacts and try to guess what they are and how they work. Encourage them to try some close observational drawings of the artefacts.

Follow-up activities
▲ Make a play corner of Sleeping Beauty's palace, with appropriate artefacts.
▲ Visit a local museum or ask a collector in for a visit.
▲ Ask parents to bring in the oldest thing they possess for a display.

Sheep shapes

Objective
Geography – to learn that sheep are farmed in different locations.

Group size
Small group or whole class.

What you need
Pictures of different sheep, a collection of woollen items and balls of wool (including natural, undyed colours) and a piece of fleece or raw wool if possible, card, paper, scissors, Sticky tape, a large map of Britain, Blu-Tack, photocopiable page 92.

Preparation
Use the photocopiable page 92 to cut out sheep shapes in card for each child. Identify a few areas on the map where sheep are farmed (such as the Lake District, South Wales and Yorkshire).

What to do
Explain that over 100 years ago, and in the story of Sleeping Beauty, most warm clothes were made from wool. Show the children the woollen items. Explain that now we have fabrics like acrylic and nylon, which are not natural fibres like wool but are made in factories.

Show the children the pictures of the different sheep and tell them that sheep are farmed, often in hilly areas and that they have strong front teeth to crop the grass that they live on. Show the children the map and mark where they live, then mark the sheep farming areas. Explain that these areas are often not suitable for growing crops but are very good for sheep rearing.

Show the examples of natural wool and explain that this has to be washed and then spun into a thread, then knitted or woven by hand or machine to make fabric. Give

each child a sheep shape and let them wind the natural wool around it to make woolly sheep of their own. These can be suspended for display or grouped on the map showing sheep farming areas.

Discussion
Ask the children what kinds of things are made from wool and tell them where wool comes from. Ask them where they would see real sheep. Talk about the features – shape, colours, ears, teeth, the way they crop grass. Ask: where would we see real sheep? and refer to the map. Stress the geographical features of hills, mountains, fields. Let them feel the woollen items and look very carefully at the threads. If you have raw wool ask: what does it feel like? What does it smell like? (You can feel and smell the lanolin oil). Then ask: how do we get different coloured wool? Explain about dyes and look at the coloured items together.

For younger children
Give these children help with winding the wool around the sheep.

For older children
Let them find the right areas on the map and fasten the sheep in place.

Follow-up activities
▲ Learn simple finger knitting.
▲ Visit a farm or zoo to see real sheep.
▲ Invite a visitor to come and give a knitting demonstration.

The briar rose hedge

Objective
Art – to paint and print simple rose patterns.

Group size
Small groups.

What you need
A reproduction of Burne-Jones 'Briar Rose' paintings (the Sleeping Beauty story in Birmingham Art Gallery or see *The Pre-Raphaelites* by Christopher Wood (Weidenfield & Nicholson Ltd)), thick paints, brushes, palettes, polystyrene pressprint sheets (supermarket meat trays for example), scissors, pencils, paper, some real roses.

What to do
Look at the paintings and talk about the Sleeping Beauty story. Look at how the artist has painted the roses and thorny hedge in great sweeping patterns, making the flowers look very real. Explain to the children that he looked at real roses to help him.

Let the children have some real roses to observe and then draw them on the paper. Next, using pencils again, ask them to draw their rose designs on to the polystyrene sheets. They can cut around the shape, then brush the paint on to the shape carefully avoiding the drawn lines which show detail. Demonstrate how to press the polystyrene on to paper to make a rose print. Make a pattern with the roses and then paint in the leaves, stalks and thorns.

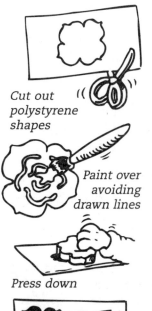

Cut out polystyrene shapes

Paint over avoiding drawn lines

Press down

Paint in leaves, stalks and thorns

Discussion
Ask the children if they can see which part of the story the artist has painted.

Can they identify who is in the painting? What colours has the artist used? What shape are the roses and the thorny hedge? What does Sleeping Beauty's dress look like? Tell them that Burne-Jones was a Victorian Pre-Raphaelite painter who painted very accurately from nature. He painted strong folds in fabric and often designed pictures for stained glass windows and tapestries. Ask the children if they can paint roses and hedges just like this artist.

For younger children
Give them help with adding paint to the polystyrene to prevent overloading.

For older children
Let them paint a group scene from Sleeping Beauty and, when dry, print the rose hedge on top.

Follow-up activities
▲ Visit an art gallery.
▲ Make a collection of flower paintings by different artists.
▲ Make roses in clay and play dough and paint them appropriately.

Lullaby

Objective
Music – to listen to music and recognise mood changes.

Group size
Whole class.

What you need
Cassette player, a recording of Tchaikovsky's 'Sleeping Beauty', a stick about 15cm long for each child with about a metre of thin, brightly coloured ribbon attached. A clear space in which to use the streamers.

Preparation
Record the 'Panorama' and 'Finale' sections (about two minutes each.)

What to do
Tell the children that Tchaikovsky was a Russian composer who lived about 100 years ago and he wrote a lot of ballet music. One of his ballets was about 'Sleeping Beauty'. He wrote his music to show the different moods of the story. Ask the children to listen carefully to the first recorded section and discuss their feelings and ideas about the music afterwards. Then play the second section and discuss the differences.

Demonstrate how the streamers can be used safely to show the feel of the music. Next let half the children have the streamers and ask them to wave them in patterns in the air to match the time and mood of the music whilst the others watch the patterns of the ribbons. Play each section again, swapping the groups around to each have a turn

Discussion
Ask the children what parts of the story the music might represent. Then inquire, which music was the faster/slower; louder/softer; gentler/stronger? How do you think that Tchaikovsky wanted the dancers to move? Then ask, how did our ribbons look? Try to emphasise the differences between the music and link it with the children's ideas for possible sections of the story. Spend time after each streamer performance asking the audience which streamer matched the music best? Why?

For younger children
Encourage them to follow your lead with the streamers.

For older children
Let them work in pairs matching each other's streamer actions.

Follow-up activities
▲ Video the streamer activity with the music.
▲ Listen to Saint Saens 'Carnival of the Animals'.
▲ Make up and tape simple tunes on class instruments to represent going to sleep and waking up.

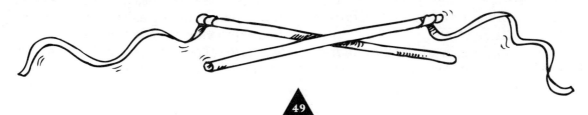

▲ 49
Starting with story
Fairy tale activities

Sleeping Beauty dance

Objective
PE – to create simple contrasting dance movements.

Group size
Whole class or groups.

What you need
The taped short sections 'Panorama' and 'Finale' from Tchaikovsky's 'Sleeping Beauty Suite' (see 'Lullaby' page 49), a large space.

Preparation
If possible, undertake 'Lullaby', page 49 before this activity.

What to do
Let the children hear the first piece of music. If they have undertaken 'Lullaby', ask them if they can remember what the music was about and who wrote it. Remind them or tell them that it was written for ballet dancers to dance the story of Sleeping Beauty.

Ask children to find a safe space and then move around in time with the music making sure they don't touch anyone else. Next play the second section and let them move again. Ask the 'audience' to identify those whose dance fits the music well. Discuss the different movements and ask children to demonstrate.

Play the music again and let the children show two different movements in their dance, such as high/low, twisting/straight, gentle/strong, using lots/little space. Let them practise their ideas and then repeat their performance.

Discussion
Focus on enabling the children to think of very different movements. Use stimulating vocabulary such as, 'I like the way John swooped high and then low,' and 'Nazreem twirled and twisted very slowly'. Ask the children watching: who was moving very quickly? Who used all the space well? Who listened well and changed their movements to match the music?

For younger children
Concentrate on only one piece of music.

For older children
Suggest that they work in pairs or threes.

Follow-up activities
▲ Beat percussion instruments in different rhythms for the children to move to.
▲ Make a whole-class dance of the people in the palace falling asleep and the thorny hedge growing all over the castle.
▲ Learn, 'The farmer's in his den', with appropriate movements.

▲ **50**
Starting with story
Fairy tale activities

Parties

Objective
RE – to explore the way important events are celebrated.

Group size
Small groups or whole class.

What you need
Three metres of string or tape, several different coloured sheets of sugar paper, sticky tape, paper, pencils, felt-tipped pens, scissors, glue and spreaders, books and pictures showing different parties and cultural celebrations.

Preparation
Cut the sugar paper into bunting shapes (as shown) and fasten it to the string. Ask the children to bring in photographs from different celebrations and parties in their families.

What to do
Ask the children to remember all the things that were celebrated in 'Sleeping Beauty' – her birth, sixteen birthdays and a wedding. Talk about celebratory parties and let the children show their photographs and speak about their family celebrations. Share your own pictures and special events. Look at the books with the children, particularly at celebrations/parties from different cultures.

Next show the children the bunting and say that they are going to label each flag with a different kind of celebration. Ask for ideas and write on the bunting: birth, naming ceremonies, birthdays, Christmas, Eid, Divali, Holi, Hanukkah, weddings, anniversaries, special successes. Talk about what these celebrations might comprise and stick photographs, drawings and pictures on each flag. Spread this activity over several sessions, gradually adding more pennants.

Discussion
Emphasise that people celebrate many similar things but also some things which are very personal to them. Share some of your own family celebrations as examples. Ask the children to hold up their photographs and ask them what's going on in this photograph? What are you celebrating? Who is at the party? Did you have a cake? Presents/games/special food/dancing/new clothes? What were they like?

For younger children
Build up the pennants and ideas over several sessions.

For older children
Let them make their own mini-bunting.

Follow-up activities
▲ Have visitors from different cultures in to talk about their celebrations.
▲ Play pass the parcel with simple forfeits.
▲ Decorate the classroom for a special celebration.

The sleeping castle

In Sleeping Beauty's castle we can see 1 sleeping Beauty, 2 dogs and 1 jester. What else can you see?

boxes fastened to wall

rose pictures

Sleeping people

tangled brown/green wool

Group size
Small groups or whole class.

What you need
A collection of different square and cuboid boxes, grey and white paper, adhesive, scissors, paint, brushes, palettes, brown and green wool, pictures of roses from catalogues (or prints from 'The briar rose hedge', page 48).

What to do
Tell the children that they are going to make a castle shape out of boxes decorated with scenes of all the people asleep inside the palace. Stick paper over the boxes to make stone shapes. Ask the children to paint the sleeping figures of Sleeping Beauty, the king and queen, courtiers, servants, and animals. Fasten the stone shapes around the display board to give a castle effect and then add the cut-out figures. Drape the wool randomly over the stones and sleepers to give the impression of the thorny hedge and stick cut out roses on top. Let some of the children write labels for the different characters in the picture, and count and write the number of different courtiers, servants, horses, dogs and so on to complete, 'In Sleeping Beauty's castle there are ... all fast asleep.'

Discussion
Explain that the boxes, large and small, are called cuboids and as the children cut and stick the covering paper, ask them to look at how many sides there are. Also ask what is the same about all the boxes, and what is different? Stress that the size can be different but the attributes – six sides, eight corners, straight sides – remain the same. Invite them to arrange the boxes in size order and compare. Discuss and choose who will paint the different characters and talk about how they might look. When you have fastened the castle stones, let the children suggest where the people should be fixed inside and where the 'hedge' should be arranged.

Follow-up activities
▲ Learn about medieval castles.
▲ Build a castle out of reclaimed boxes.
▲ Plant a rose bush and care for it.

Sleeping Beauty's crib

Group size
Small groups.

What you need
A large cardboard box, about two metres of plain material (old net curtains are useful), several large sheets of card, sticks, foil roll inners or tightly rolled newspaper, sticky tape, thick paint, brushes, old plates, foam sponges, newspaper to cover tables.

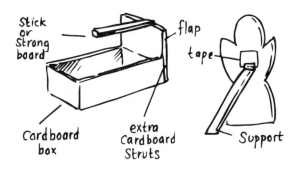

Preparation
Make the crib from the cardboard box as shown. Cut the fabric into a length for draping over the crib and for sheets and covers, spread them out flat over a pad of newspaper. Cut the foam sponges into shapes associated with the story – roses, spinning wheels, fairy figures, crowns.

What to do
Explain to the children that they are going to make a three-dimensional display of Sleeping Beauty's birth celebrations. Tip a little paint on to a plate, press the sponge into this and test print this on to paper, then when the children are happy, use it to print a pattern on to the fabric. Paint large figures of the 13 fairies on to card. When dry, cut them out and fasten a support at the back to make them stand up round the crib. Put a doll in the crib and assemble the scene.

Discussion
Ask the children what shapes, patterns and colours they will choose. Ask them to test their ideas first and discuss together how well they look. When painting the fairies ask: how will your fairy be different to the others? What colours and clothes will she wear? Ensure you only get one bad fairy!

Follow-up activities
▲ Learn a lullaby song.
▲ Ask a parent with a young baby to bring the child into school.
▲ Look at some designs used for children's wallpapers, bedding and rooms.

Celebration biscuits

Group size
Small groups.

What you need
Packets of digestive, ginger nut and shortbread biscuits, icing sugar, a lemon and squeezer, blackcurrant cordial, water, food colourings, mixing bowls, forks and spreaders, 'hundreds and thousands' and other cake decorations (chocolate buttons or raisins). *Avoid anything that might cause choking.*

Preparation
Decorate some biscuits as examples.

What to do
Talk about cakes and party treats and look at the range of biscuits and decorations. Explain that you are going to make some biscuits for Sleeping Beauty's wedding and show them the ones which you've already decorated. Explain that you need icing to fix all the decorations in place. Help them squeeze the lemons and mix the juice with enough sugar to make a buttery consistency. Repeat with the blackcurrant cordial and also with plain water adding a few drops of food colouring to provide a variety. Spread the icing on to the biscuits and let the children choose their decorations, sprinkling them or arranging them carefully to make pictures and patterns. Leave them to dry out. Share them together later!

Discussion
Ask the children why people enjoy celebrating special events and what sort of food they enjoy. Ask: why are party treats different to everyday food? What should Sleeping Beauty's wedding biscuits look like? Ask the children to look carefully at the biscuit sizes, (smallest, bigger, biggest) colours, shapes, (square, circle, rectangle) and the decorations and ask them to say why they make their choices. Ask them to compare and describe their patterns with friends. Help them to decide how they will set out the biscuits to serve them. Make sure they test the biscuits and describe the taste!

For younger children
Help them spread the icing and limit the choice of decorations.

For older children
Ask them to draw their designs first and use these for reference. Encourage them to work out how they will serve them and how many each one will get.

Follow-up activities
▲ Make paper doilies and serviettes.
▲ Make sweets for Divali and Eid celebrations.
▲ Write a class recipe for making the biscuits with drawings and instructions.

Cinderella

The story of Cinderella can be traced back to a Chinese version around 850 AD, yet its message is just as fresh to young children today who can delight in Cinderella's magical transformation and enjoy the comforting idea of fairy godmothers! This beautiful tale also gives opportunities to develop a range of mathematical and language activities, to explore Cinderella going to the ball through music, art, PE, cookery and geography work, and also provides ideas for science, history, design and technology and RE.

Cinderella's father had remarried after her mother died and although he loved Cinderella dearly, her new step-mother treated her badly. Her own unpleasant daughters lived lazy lives, whilst beautiful Cinderella worked in the kitchen, treated worse than a servant. Her step-sisters lived in comfort but poor Cinderella wore only shabby rags and lived on scraps.

One day an invitation from the prince arrived, inviting everyone to a grand ball at the palace. The ugly sisters prepared for the great event, but Cinderella had to stay at home. The sisters left in a flurry of satin and silk leaving Cinderella to weep alone.

Suddenly there was a flash of light and a kindly lady appeared saying, 'Don't cry Cinderella, for I am your fairy godmother and you shall go to the ball!' Cinderella watched as the lovely fairy wove her magic, turning a pumpkin into a golden coach, six mice into fine horses and several frogs into a uniformed driver and coachmen. She touched Cinderella with her silver wand and the rags changed into a glittering ball gown, and on her bare feet she wore crystal slippers.

'Just one thing,' said the fairy godmother 'you must leave the ball before midnight because at twelve o'clock everything will change back to normal!'

Cinderella cried, 'I shan't forget!' and raced away in her coach. She was the most beautiful girl at the ball and the young prince danced every single dance with her. Suddenly she heard midnight striking on the clock and she fled, losing one of her magical shoes in her rush.

The prince had fallen in love with Cinderella and he vowed to find the beautiful stranger and make her his wife. Servants carried the glass slipper from house to house for the prince knew it would fit only his love. The prince watched as the ugly sisters tried the slipper on in vain. 'Who else lives here?' he asked forlornly. 'Only Cinderella,' answered the sisters. When she tried the magic slipper on it fitted perfectly!

The prince was overjoyed and they were married at the greatest wedding anyone could remember.

Invitation to the ball

Objective
English – to make simple invitations.

Group size
Small groups or whole class.

What you need
An A2 sheet of paper, an A4 sheet of paper for each child, about 20cm of brightly coloured thin ribbon for each child, pencils, felt-tipped pens.

Preparation
Write out the following invitation words on the large sheet of paper 'His Royal Highness Prince Charming requests the pleasure of the company of ...(leave a blank line) at his Grand Ball on ...(fill in the actual date) RSVP', add some decoration such as crowns. Roll it into a scroll and tie it with ribbon. Photocopy the same wording on to each child's sheet and leave spaces for them to fill in name, date and decoration.

His Royal Highness requests the pleasure of the company of

– – – – – – – – – –

at his Grand Ball on

– – – – – – – – – –

R·S·V·P

What to do
Explain that we have invitations for many things – birthday parties, weddings, parties. Unroll the large invitation and say this is an invitation like Cinderella and her sisters received from the prince. Read it aloud, pointing to the words. When you get to the space, ask whose name should go there and fill it in sounding out the phonics as you go. Explain what RSVP means ('Repondez s'il vous plait' – please reply). Show the children the decoration and clues that it came from a prince.

Give the children their own sheets and ask them to fill in their names and copy the date. They can add decorations and when it's complete, roll it up and fasten the ribbon.

Discussion
Talk about invitations they might send or receive, and about the sort of things they say and how they are decorated. Talk about how scrolls were used by messengers before the post was established.

For younger children
Let them copy from name cards and help them tie the ribbons.

For older children
Write replies to the invitation.

Follow-up activities
▲ Make a collection of invitations and replies.
▲ Write and invite a visitor into the class or group.
▲ Make a Post Office play area.

The Grand Ball menu

Objective
English – to know writing is used for lists and menus.

Group size
Small groups.

What you need
An A2 sheet of paper, A4 sheets of card for each child, strips of card about 5cm x 10cm, pictures of different foods (magazines and adverts), sticky tape, scissors, glue, spreaders, felt-tipped pens, pencils.

Preparation
Fold the paper in half and label the front 'Menu for the Prince's Grand Ball'. Cut out pictures or drawings of some food (such as chips, jellies, samosas, stews, oriental food, pies) and mount them on the card strips, write in the names. Fold the children's A4 sheets in half.

What to do
Explain that at the Grand Ball there was a menu to say what food was served, and in what order, to Cinderella and the guests. Tell the children they are going to make up menus showing what they would like to eat at the Grand Ball. Show them your large menu, read the title, open it up. Now show them the food cards one by one, reading the labels, and ask the children to think which ones they will choose for their menu. Have blanks to use for any new foods they might suggest. Discuss the order of the courses and use sticky tape to secure them loosely in place as an example.

Distribute the menu cards, food cards, magazines, glue spreaders and scissors and let the children choose their own feast, cutting and sticking pictures or copying the words. Finally they can decorate their menus.

Discussion
Ask the children to think of all their favourite foods. Ask them what they serve for visitors at home. What special drinks could we have? Encourage them to talk about their own party food. Ask them: which will be served first/second/last? Encourage the children to explain why they have chosen their own menus.

For younger children
When younger children have chosen their pictures, add the words for them.

For older children
Let them complete their writing in their own words.

Follow-up activities
▲ Make up a menu for a real class party.
▲ Make a play corner restaurant and café with menus, bills and so on.
▲ Use a computer to print out menus and price lists.

Does it fit?

Objective
Mathematics – to look at different sizes and measurements.

Group size
Small group.

What you need
A collection of different sized and styled footwear, large clothes pegs, paper, pencils, crayons, a line chart to show different foot sizes (see diagram), scissors, glue, spreaders.

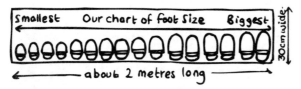

Preparation
Make the chart as shown.

What to do
Talk about Cinderella's glass slipper and what it might have looked like and felt like to wear. Bring out shoes from your collection and put them in a heap. Ask the children to sort them into pairs and peg them together. Count the pairs and also show the children how they can be counted in twos. Remind the children of how people tried on Cinderella's slipper, then pick children and ask them to select shoes they think will fit them. Let others have turns to guess. Discuss different foot sizes.

Show the chart and say they are going to show their foot sizes on it. Demonstrate how to draw round their feet (in shoes). Let them work in pairs to draw round each other's feet, they can then colour the shape, and cut it out. Stick them in size order on to the line chart.

Discussion
As each child looks for a shoe that fits, ask them to look at their own foot and measure it against each possible choice. Involve the group saying: is it too big, too small or about right? Ask the children: what sort of shoe is it? Who would wear it? Look at fastenings, heel, colour and so on. When placing the shoe templates in order, ask: is this bigger than this one? Where will it go on the line?

For younger children
Provide some very small and very large shoes to help in ordering the sizes.

For older children
Let them try to order the shoe sizes themselves; discuss findings.

Follow-up activities
▲ Visit a shoe shop and use a foot measure.
▲ Set up a shoe shop play area.
▲ Collect and learn about specialist footwear (flippers, wellies and ballet shoes).

Cinderella's day

Objective
Mathematics – to learn that hours are a measure of time.

Group size
Small group or whole class.

What you need
A large clock face, 'Cinderella's day' chart drawn as shown with eight pairs of cardboard clock hands fastened with paper fasteners, a cut-out figure of Cinderella (see photocopiable page 93).

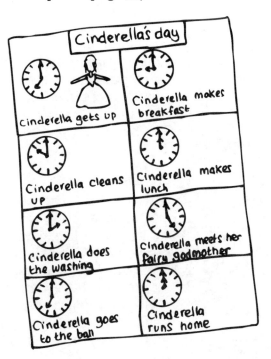

What to do
Refer to the story and talk about what Cinderella did on the day of the Grand Ball. Emphasise getting up, making breakfast, cleaning the house, making lunch for the ugly sisters, doing the washing, then meeting her fairy godmother, going to the ball, running home at midnight amongst other suggestions.

Show the children the chart, put the Cinderella cut-out in the first box and point to each word and read it out. Show them the clock face and discuss the time that Cinderella may have done the various things. Move the clock hands to the time required and ask a child to come and fix the hands on the chart to show the same time, asking the others to check and carefully count the hours and point out the position of the hour and minutes hands to reinforce time-telling. Repeat for all the boxes. Count the hours between Cinderella's activities, for example, find out how long she stayed at the ball.

For younger children
Choose the times for Cinderella's day and help them with the positioning of the hands.

For older children
Stamp clock faces on to individual charts and let them copy or complete the times of Cinderella's day for themselves.

Follow-up activities
▲ Learn the times of the school or playgroup activities on clock faces.
▲ Learn to sing 'My grandfather's clock'.
▲ Make clock music, playing and counting the hours striking.

Listen!

Objective
Science – to learn that different things make different sounds.

Group size
Small groups or whole class.

What you need
A tape recorder, a tape of everyday sounds, a collection of everyday objects on a tray – saucepan and wooden spoon, knives and forks, jug of water and beaker, potato, chopping board and knife, bell, scrubbing brush, pictures of a mouse, a frog, a clock and the Grand Ball.

Preparation
Make a short tape of different everyday household sounds such as Cinderella might have heard as she laboured away in her house: mixing in a bowl, scrubbing something, chopping up vegetables and a bell ringing for attention. Provide the same everyday objects in your collection. Add 'mice' squeaking, 'frogs' croaking, a snatch of dance music and a clock striking midnight.

What to do
Explain that when Cinderella was alone in her kitchen she would have heard lots of different sounds, and that you have made a tape of some of them. Tell them to listen carefully, and play the tape through once, then play it again stopping after each sound asking them to guess what it might be. Produce the tray of items, play the tape again asking individuals to match the things which might be making the sound and

demonstrate them (only adults should demonstrate the chopping). After each guess ask the children how the sound is made, for example banging, rubbing. Explain that all sounds travel by invisible waves that come through the air and are caught by our ears and are heard inside our heads. *Stress that hearing can be damaged by putting things in ears.* Play the tape again, and retell the story, stopping after each sound, letting the children say what Cinderella is doing.

Discussion
As you play each sound ask the children what it sounds like. What do you think is making this sound? Is it loud or soft? What might be going on? As each object is used, ask what can you hear happening? How is this sound made?

For younger children
Restrict the number of sounds and objects or split the activity into two sessions.

For older children
Make a taped sound story of Cinderella, interspersing the story with sound effects.

Follow-up activities
▲ Have a silent listening minute at different times of the day and identify the sounds.
▲ Look at different animals' ears.
▲ Experiment with different musical instruments.

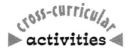

The search for Cinderella

Objective
Design and Technology – to make a container for the glass slipper.

Group size
Small group or whole class in groups.

What you need
A range of reclaimed materials (cardboard boxes of different shapes and sizes, tubes, egg and cheese boxes), card, string, paper, plastic and polythene bags, fabric scraps, foil, ribbons and trimmings, wool, pipe cleaners, glue, sticky tape, paper, pencils, paint, brushes. A play 'glass slipper' to test the products.

What to do
Remind the children of the part of the story when the prince's men carry the precious glass slipper from house to house to search for Cinderella. Explain that they would need a strong, safe container in which to carry the fragile slipper but that it would be a very important looking and regal affair! Discuss what it might have been like and emphasise the need to provide a secure container.

Ask the children to draw their plans on paper and then use these to help them choose reclaimed materials and construct their model. Test the containers with a play 'glass slipper'!

Discussion
Look at each child's plans and ask them to explain to others how it works. Ask: how is the slipper kept safe? How easy is it to get out to try on? Is it the right size? How can we tell it is from the prince? What colour will it be when you've finished it? Encourage the other children to ask questions and make suggestions. Also, ask: how will you join this together? Will you need glue or sticky tape for this plastic/foil/fabric? How can you cover it/paint it/decorate it?

For younger children
Let younger children experiment with the materials without drawing plans.

For older children
Let them use the test 'slipper' regularly and adapt and improve their models, explaining their reasons to other children.

Follow-up activities
▲ Make magic slippers out of clay or Plasticine.
▲ Make a model coach from a pumpkin.
▲ Sew a simple cushion for Cinderella's golden coach or royal throne.

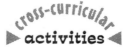

Why did it happen?

Objective
History – to look at how some actions affect things (cause and effect).

Group size
Small groups or whole class.

What you need
Large sheets of card for labels, felt-tipped pens.

Preparation
Make labels saying: 'Why did this happen?' and 'Because'.

What to do
Tell the children that in the story of Cinderella certain things happened which resulted in other things happening. Explain that if the fairy godmother had been on holiday that day she couldn't have helped Cinderella and given her a golden coach and her lovely dress!

Retell the story, stopping at suitable places (Cinderella had a new stepmother, the stepmother treated her own daughters better than Cinderella, only the ugly sisters were going to the ball and so on). Display and ask the question, 'Why did this happen?'. Then ask the children to suggest answers taking turns to hold up 'Because' as they give their answers.

Discussion
Stress that things might have been different, suggest some possibilities and ask the children to think of some. For instance, what would have happened if the stepmother had been kinder, Cinderella hadn't left at midnight or didn't lose her shoe? Stretch the children's imagination but emphasise the cause and effect of happenings.

For younger children
Help them with suggestions for why things happened and how they would be different in other circumstances.

For older children
Let them tell the 'alternative' Cinderella story where things happen very differently.

Follow-up activities
▲ Look at other fairy stories and change the endings.
▲ Make a 'Why did this happen?' book.
▲ Find out about things which have changed in the locality such as buildings pulled down, the introduction of 'park and ride', new traffic lights/roads and so on.

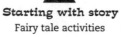

Going to the ball

Objective
Geography – to look at simple journeys turning left and right.

Group size
Small groups.

What you need
A large pair of mittens/gloves, two pieces of card 5cm x 8cm, two small sticky labels for each child, red and green felt-tipped pens, pencils, photocopiable page 94.

Preparation
Label the large cards 'left' (red) and 'right' (green) and attach them to the correct mitten. Label the sticky labels in the same way.

What to do
Explain that Cinderella had to make a journey to the palace for the ball and at some places she would have had to turn left or right to get there. Put the gloves on yourself and turn slightly so your hands match the children's, then show the children the left and right signs. Ask the children to wave their right arms, then left arms, following your lead. Lightly attach a sticky label on the back of each child's hands and repeat the actions, letting them use the labels to help.

Next give out the photocopiable sheet and pencils. Explain that as Cinderella was travelling down the road in her golden coach she would come to road junctions where she had to decide which way to go. Show the children how to turn their sheets as if they were walking along the road. Let them draw in a line but stop at each junction.

Show the gloves again and discuss whether she must go left or right. If Cinderella goes left, ask them to put an 'l' for left or 'r' for right, then continue the journey and draw in the line as they go. Work slowly together to get the idea of left and right.

Discussion
Talk about how they turn left and right moving round their classroom or building. When Cinderella needs to make a turn, refer to the map and check everyone is at the same place, and ask the children to point the direction she must go. Ask: which hand is it, left or right?

For younger children
Enlarge Cinderella's journey map and work together as a group on this.

For older children
Let older children design their own journeys, indicating whether Cinderella must go left or right.

Follow-up activities
▲ Make a big map of the locality and plot in the children's journeys to school.
▲ Play 'Hunt the slipper' saying left or right instead of 'hot' and 'cold'.
▲ Learn the Green Cross Code and talk about road safety.

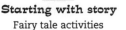

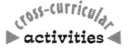

Dressed for the ball!

Objective
Art – to design and make Cinderella's costume.

Group size
Small groups or whole class.

What you need
Fabric scraps of a variety of materials, ribbons and trimmings, sequins and beads, glue and spreaders, photocopiable page 93, one per child.

Preparation
Mount the sheets on to card (optional).

What to do
Tell the children that they are going to dress Cinderella for the ball. Show them the kinds of fabric available and also the trimmings. Let the children choose their fabrics and decide how to decorate Cinderella.

Hand out a copy of the photocopiable sheet to the children and let them cut out their chosen fabrics and stick them on to the figure. When complete these can be cut out to use for display or left on the sheet.

Discussion
Ask the children to look carefully at the fabrics before they make their choices. Ask them, what sort of material would Cinderella's dress be made of? What colours would she wear? Which materials have you chosen? How does it feel – rough or smooth or silky or heavy or light? Is it a good material to dance in? How will you make it look like a magic dress?

For younger children
Help them with cutting out the fabric shapes and sticking small beads.

For older children
Cut out the figure and ask them to show Cinderella in her rags on one side and Cinderella dressed for the ball on the back.

Follow-up activities
▲ Bring in party dresses and look at the different materials and styles.
▲ Make a tiara or crown from card and coloured foil, beads and sequins.
▲ Ask a parent to bring in their sewing or embroidery to show the children.

Waltz time

Objective
Music – to learn waltz time pulse (3/4 time).

Group size
Whole class.

What you need
A tape or record of a ballroom waltz (choose ballroom dance music because of the strict tempo throughout, Viennese waltzes tend to speed up). A selection of drums, beaters and other percussion instruments, sufficient space to move.

What to do
Explain that there would have been lots of waltzes at the grand ball and Cinderella and the prince would have danced round with Cinderella's beautiful dress twirling out as she spun in time with the music. Play part of the tape and ask the children to listen carefully to the beat, often provided by drums, percussion or double bass. Then play it again gently clapping the 'one–two–three' pattern of the beat, asking the children to join in with you.

Make the first beat slightly stronger than the others 'ONE–two–three'. Stop the tape and practise, then accompany the music again. When the beat is established let the children play the rhythm on different instruments. If space allows, let the children dance round the room following your lead turning slowly in time with the music.

Discussion
Ask, can you hear the lowest notes beating a steady rhythm? What other instruments can you hear? What instruments might you choose to keep the steady rhythm? Ask the children if the music makes them feel like dancing. How might you move in your dance? Explain that many people enjoy ballroom dancing and a waltz is one of the favourite slow dances.

For younger children
Use short sections of the tape at a time, and help the children clap the rhythm.

For older children
Play other waltzes (for example 'The skater's waltz' by Waldteufel or Tchaikovsky's 'Waltz of the Flowers') and let them clap the beat (these are often much faster).

Follow-up activities
▲ Play 'follow my leader' using different rhythms on percussion instruments.
▲ Make up simple dances in pairs and groups to the waltz time.
▲ Invite visitors in to demonstrate ballroom dancing.

Travelling

Objective
PE – to move in different ways using different parts of the body.

Group size
Small groups or whole class.

What you need
A large space, a small drum or tambourine.

What to do
Remind the children that the fairy godmother changed mice and frogs into horses and frogs. Discuss how these different animals move and what parts of their bodies they use.

Ask the children to find a space and move like mice, horses and people. Use certain children to demonstrate interesting movements. Now say that you will be the fairy godmother and when you make your magic spell, using your instrument, they have to change from mice to horses and back again when they hear the magic again, telling them to change slowly then quickly. Similarly, let them change from frogs to people and back. Now let the children choose other animals and change from one to another as you indicate. Next ask them to work in pairs, choosing to be any animals and copying each other's movements. Guess which animals they have chosen.

Discussion
Ask the children: how many legs have the animals got? How do they move? What do their legs/arms/paws/heads/tails do? When the children choose their own animals ask them if they can show by their own movements what they are? Tell us how your legs/arms/head/body is moving like a...? Develop questioning skills by encouraging the other children to ask questions such as: how many legs have you got? Do you have a long tail? (rather than random guessing).

For younger children
Suggest different animals which they might be such as cats, snakes, fish, birds, elephants or giraffes.

For older children
Ask them to make up a short sequence of movements changing from mice to horses to frogs to people, practise it and perform it.

Follow-up activities
▲ Make animal masks to wear.
▲ Learn about tadpoles and frogs.
▲ Learn to sing 'Five little speckled frogs'.

Weddings

Objective
RE – to learn about different wedding celebrations.

Group size
Small group or whole class.

What you need
Wedding dresses and associated artefacts (photographs, invitations, cards, garlands) from a variety of cultures – or a book with information and illustrations. If possible invite visitors from different cultures in to talk about their wedding celebrations. Paper, pencils, sugar paper, glue and spreaders.

Preparation
Ask the parents to bring in photographs of any family weddings, bridesmaids outfits or special clothing. Fold sugar paper to make a simple book.

What to do
Talk about Cinderella and the prince getting married and what the ceremony and celebration might be like. Ask the children if they have ever been to a wedding, seen one on television or seen wedding photographs. Explain that people often wear special clothes for the occasion, tell them that white wedding dresses in Britain are a Victorian invention, and that many Asian brides often wear red. Be very sensitive to the fact that many children have parents who have not chosen to marry but explain that many couples do wish to marry and if they do, they make promises in public to stay together and care for each other.

Show some of the artefacts that you have collected and let some of the children wear any wedding apparel, share the books together or let the visitors share their experiences. Let the children draw a picture of Cinderella's wedding to the prince in any way they choose. Stick them in the class book.

Discussion
Ask the children about weddings they may have attended, ask if any of them have been a bridesmaid or a page boy. If so, what did they wear? What did they have to do? What happened in the church/temple/mosque/synagogue? What happened afterwards at the party? Talk about Silver/Ruby/Golden wedding anniversaries.

For younger children
Introduce only two contrasting wedding customs at a time.

For older children
Let them write a sentence to accompany their wedding illustration.

Follow-up activities
▲ Hold a 'mock' wedding in class and let the children take different parts.
▲ Have a wedding dressing-up corner with different cultural outfits.
▲ Watch a wedding video.

Ladies at the ball

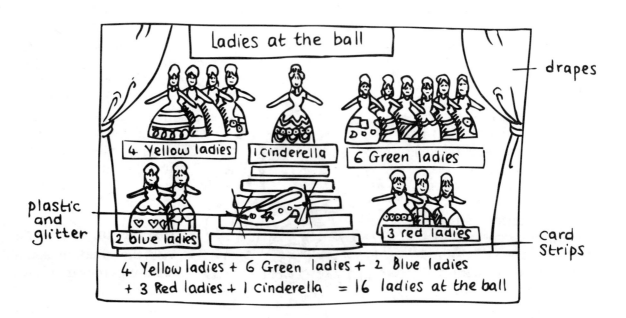

Group size
Small groups.

What you need
Cut-out figures of Cinderella (photocopiable page 93), fabric scraps, trimmings, beads, card, backing paper, scissors, glue, spreaders, a picture of an elegant shoe, polythene or clear plastic, glitter, fabric for draperies.

Preparation
Back the display board and drape fabric. Cut a strip of card 1cm x 32cm, then ten more, reducing the length by 2cm each time. Stick these on to make a staircase design. Trace the shoe shape on to the polythene or plastic and cut it out, cover with glue and sprinkle with glitter to make the 'glass slipper'. Sort the fabric and trimmings into colour groupings.

What to do
Let the children work in groups of different sizes, each using a different colour. Invite the children to stick fabric on to the cut-out lady figures, adding glitter and trimmings to match. Arrange the finished figures around the display and label each group: '6 ladies dressed in blue' and so on. Let one child make Cinderella dressed in white and silver and put her at the top of the staircase as though she is fleeing. Let the children choose where the glass slipper will have fallen and a title for you to label the whole display. Add an addition sum, for example, '6 green ladies + 4 yellow ladies + Cinderella = 11 ladies at the ball.'

Discussion
Encourage the children to look at the 'staircase' and ask them if they can see the longest/shortest/middle-sized stair, count them together to check. Ask the children how many different shades of blue they can see, and ask them to identify the darkest/lightest blue. What other things are this colour blue? Ask, how many ladies are there in the blue group? How many do you think there are altogether?

Follow-up activities
▲ Go for a walk to find and count different steps and stairs.
▲ Set up colour tables, changing the colour each week.
▲ Make and decorate paper fans to have at the ball.

When midnight comes

Group size
Small groups.

What you need
A collection of flat boxes (chocolates, tissues), a cheese box, sticky tape, adhesive, paper, paint, brushes, bright and dull backing paper, felt-tipped pens, photocopiable page 93, clear polythene or plastic, glitter, a picture of an elegant shoe.

Preparation
Divide the display board into two. Back one half in bright paper the other in dull. Enlarge the picture of Cinderella (photocopiable page 93) and draw a faint line down the middle.

What to do
Working in groups, ask children to prepare different parts of the changing scene of Cinderella's story. Let one group arrange the boxes to make a grandfather clock, using the cheese box as the face. Draw in the dial showing midnight, tape the boxes together, paint them and fasten the clock between the two halves of the display.

Another group can paint the banquet scene and the ball (tables, food, dancers, golden coach) and another group could work on the kitchen (fireplace, dark old furniture, mice, frogs). A further group can paint Cinderella, half in a ball gown and half in ragged clothes. Assemble the pictures and fix them to the display. Add the glass slipper in a suitable place. Let the children choose a title for you to label the display.

Discussion
Encourage the children to talk about the part of the story they are illustrating and ask, what changes will happen when midnight comes? How is the other side of the display going to be different to yours? Stress the details that will change such as Cinderella's hair, her shoes and so on.

Follow-up activities
▲ Find out about people who work at night.
▲ Read *Six Dinner Sid* by Inga Moore (Simon and Schuster Young Books) and how he changed from house to house.
▲ Make a collection of different clocks, watches and timers.

When midnight comes everything will change back
cheese box
boxes
children's paintings

▲ 69
Starting with story
Fairy tale activities

Jelly for a banquet

Group size
Very small groups.

What you need
Packets of jelly (different colours and flavours), a kettle, measuring jug, a bowl for each jelly, balloon whisks or forks, jelly moulds, access to a fridge, fruit, a knife and chopping board. A chart ruled into boxes and labelled.

Preparation
Ask the children to wash their hands, and wash the fruit.

What to do
Explain that the group is going to make special jellies fit for a banquet at the Grand Ball. Demonstrate how you chop up the fruit always stressing that knives are dangerous so only adults should use them. Let the children arrange the chopped fruit in the jelly moulds. Make up the jelly, one flavour at a time, according to the instructions, letting the children watch safely. The safest method is to dissolve the jelly in very hot water (half the total water required) then top it up with the same amount of cold water. Show them how you measure this. Let the children stir this gently to mix it thoroughly then pour it carefully into the jelly moulds. Put the jellies into the fridge to set. Complete the recipe chart, acting as scribe for their ideas. When ready to serve, dip the moulds into a bowl of quite hot water for a few seconds, invert on a plate, shake, pray and de-mould! Share them together at the class banquet.

Discussion
Let the children break up the jelly and describe what it feels like. Ask the children what they think will happen when the hot water goes on to the jelly, ask them to watch carefully and to say what is happening as you stir. Ask them where the jelly has gone. Introduce the word 'dissolved' and explain that although the jelly will set, it won't be the same as it was. When the jelly is poured into the moulds ask them what is happening to the fruit. When you de-mould the jellies ask them to say what it

sounds like and looks like on the plate. How is it different to the packet of jelly?

Follow-up activities
▲ Lay the tables with the right number of mats, bowls and spoons, learn to serve.
▲ Make banquet food in play dough and Plasticine for a dolls' feast.
▲ Sing 'Jelly on the plate', *This Little Puffin*, compiled by Elizabeth Matterson (Puffin).

► introduction ◄

Little Red Riding Hood

Red Riding Hood is a classic fairy story, a triumph of good over evil woven into a simple adventure that young children can easily identify with. It also provides a framework for a stimulating educational programme in English, mathematics and science and exciting activities in history, geography, RE, technology and cookery.

One day Red Riding Hood's mother called her and said, 'I want you to take these goodies to Granny as she hasn't been well and they will help her get better.' Red Riding Hood was delighted, she loved her kind, old granny and she wanted to help her. 'Now go through the woods, keep on the path, don't wander off it and don't talk to any strangers,' said her mother.

Red Riding Hood put on her lovely warm, scarlet cloak, picked up her basket and set off from their house, turning to wave at her mother. She walked on and she saw her friend the woodcutter. 'Hello Red Riding Hood,' he said, 'where are you going today?'

'I'm off to visit my granny. She isn't too well and I'm taking these tasty things to make her better,' she replied. The woodcutter smiled. 'Off you go now,' he told her 'But stick to the path, for I hear the Big Bad Wolf is about again.'

Red Riding Hood laughed, 'I'm not afraid of him!' and she went on her way. But the wolf had been snoozing behind a tree and had overheard their conversation. Swiftly he galloped off ahead of Red Riding Hood and crept into granny's house. Poor granny saw the Wolf and ran away, shutting herself in the cupboard.

Soon Red Riding Hood arrived and knocked at the door. 'Granny it's me, can I come in?' The Wolf called out in a crackly voice, 'Lift the latch and come in, my dear!' Red Riding Hood went in and put her basket down on Granny's bed where the Wolf had crept, dressing himself in Granny's frilly cap and night-dress. Red Riding Hood was puzzled by her granny's face and said 'Granny, what big eyes you have!'

'All the better to see you with, my dear!' replied the Wolf.

'And what big ears you have!'

'All the better to hear you with' smirked the Wolf.

'But Granny,' persisted Red Riding Hood, 'what big teeth you have!'

'All the better to EAT you with!' growled the Wolf, leaping from the bed.

Red Riding Hood screamed and fled from the house with the Wolf chasing her. But the woodcutter had heard the commotion and had come running through the trees, and he soon chased the wicked Wolf right away. Red Riding Hood and Granny and the brave woodcutter all sat down and shared the tasty picnic together, knowing that the Wolf was gone forever.

Dear Granny...

Objective
English – to write a simple letter.

Group size
Small groups.

What you need
Samples of real letters which you have received together with their envelopes, paper, plain envelopes, pencils, sticky paper rectangles (about 2cm x 3cm), two A2 sheets of paper, felt-tipped pens.

Preparation
Make an envelope by cutting one of the A2 sheets into a square and folding.

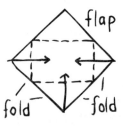

What to do
Explain that Red Riding Hood's mother would have written to Granny to say that her granddaughter was going to visit her. Talk about the types of letters which people write and show your examples, first looking at the envelope (name, address, stamp) and then the letter (address, date, the layout). Emphasise that the print/handwriting conveys a message.

Discuss together what Red Riding Hood might write to her granny, then act as scribe and using an A2 sheet write down the children's ideas for Red Riding Hood's address, the date and a short note. Put the children's ideas for Granny's address on the envelope.

Let the children write or copy the letter and address their envelopes. Give them the sticky paper and ask them to draw a 'stamp' of their own and affix it to their envelope.

Discussion
Ask the children, do you have letters in your house? Who brings them? What sort of letters does your family get? Use your examples and say: can you see the address/date/the names of who sent the letter and who received the letter? Talk about different stamp designs and ask if the children know why the Queen's head is on all British stamps?

For younger children
Write the words on their letters for copy writing.

For older children
Let them write their own messages.

Follow-up activities
▲ Write real letters, stamp and post them.
▲ Send the children a 'reply' from granny.
▲ Make a visit to the Post Office.

Story puppets

Objective
English – to act out a story using simple puppets.

Group size
Small groups.

What you need
Card, peasticks or equivalent, sticky tape, felt-tipped pens, crayons/coloured pencils, wool and fabric scraps, pencils, glue, spreaders, scissors, enlarged pictures of the characters and their eyes (photocopiable page 96).

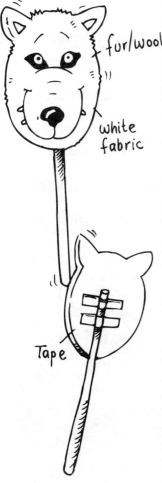

fur/wool

white fabric

Tape

Preparation
Enlarge photocopiable page 96 to show to the children. Make an example of a stick puppet. Cut out oval head shapes from the card.

What to do
Explain to the children that they are going to make puppets to act out the story of Red Riding Hood. Show them the puppet you have made and talk about how you made it. Point out the character illustrations and eyes to give them some ideas.

Let the children draw their character's face on the oval card, colouring it in and adding wool 'fur' and hair, they could add simple cloaks and hats to complete their puppets. Tape the masks to the sticks.

Encourage the children to make up parts of the story, holding the puppets up to act it out. They can then perform their final versions to the other children.

Discussion
Talk about which characters will be needed and let them choose which one to make. Ask the group: how can we make the puppet look like the wolf/woodcutter/Granny? What colours/materials can we use? When acting out the story say: what sort of voice would she have – high/low, loud/soft, gentle/harsh? How would the Wolf change his voice when he was trying to be Granny?

For younger children
Help them to fasten the costumes and masks to the sticks.

For older children
Let them work out the scenes for themselves.

Follow-up activities
▲ Make a table-top puppet theatre and make simple scenery.
▲ Listen to the story of *Pinnochio* (Ladybird).

Visiting Granny

Objective
Mathematics – to count and match corresponding numbers.

Group size
Small groups.

What you need
Photocopiable page 95, one for each child, large dice – labelled with dots from 0-3, counters.

What to do
Tell the group that they are going to play a counting game to see who can get Red Riding Hood to her granny first. Each child takes a turn to throw the dice, counting the number thrown and then moving the correct number of squares on the sheet. The first one home wins!

Discussion
Count the squares together to start with and then say, let's watch and see if s/he moves the right number of squares. Or say let's all count together to help. As each character is reached on the board ask: who is this? What did they do in the story?

For younger children
Enlarge the photocopiable sheet to make one large board for the whole group to play together (in two teams) and use dice with dots to help counting.

For older children
Use dice with numerals.

Follow-up activities
▲ Mark out a number track on the playground and play a dice game with children as 'counters'.

▲ Practise counting skills using number lines.

▲ Make up board games with forfeits for some squares.

Where's the wolf?

Objective
Mathematics – to learn about position.

Group size
Small group or whole class.

What you need
A collection of small everyday items (mug, book, pencils, plant), a picture of the wolf, card, felt-tipped pens.

Preparation
Make card labels saying: **under, on, behind, in front of, near, far away, next to**, using a pen in one colour. Make a label for each object using another colour print. Make a card strip which says, 'The wolf is hiding…'.

What to do
Explain that the wolf was hiding in the woods to spy on Red Riding Hood and that you are going to play a game to find where he is hiding now.

Show the children the objects, place them where they can be seen and put their labels next to them. Produce your picture of the wolf and place him amongst the items. Ask: where is the wolf hiding? Let children take turns to hide the wolf and also to say where he is, using the positional language. Complete the sentence card using the correct titles and positions, reading them together.

Discussion
Say: where's the wolf hiding now? Remind the children of the choices by asking: is he **under** the cup? **On** the book? **Behind** the plant? and so on, stressing the positional term.

For younger children
Restrict the number of objects.

For older children
Let them draw and label different hiding places in books or on paper.

Follow-up activities
▲ Play 'Hide and seek' outside.
▲ Play 'Kim's Game' with objects on a tray.
▲ Make clay and Plasticine models of the wolf.

What big eyes you have!

· Objective

Science – to learn that living things have different eye characteristics.

Group size
Small groups or whole class.

What you need
Photocopiable page 96 for each child, pictures of different animals (mammals, birds, insects, reptiles, fish), pencils.

What to do
Remind the children of how Red Riding Hood spoke to the wicked wolf who was dressed as Granny saying: 'What big ears/eyes/teeth you have!'. Tell them that they are going to look at different types of eyes.

Show the pictures one by one, talking about the similarities and differences of the eyes. Use the correct classification word (for example, reptile) to reinforce similarities of specific groups. Give out the sheets and let the children match the eyes to their owners.

Discussion
Talk about the different parts of the eyes – the pupils, irises, eyelids, eyelashes (or lack of them) and ask or explain what they are used for. Ask: what do our eyelids do? When do we close them? Have all animals got eyelashes? Can we see them? Are all the pupils the same shape? What about the size? Are our eyes all the same colour? Are there different colours in the animals' eyes?

For younger children
Draw their attention to the differences and help them select the matching pairs on the sheet.

For older children
Cut out the matching pairs and group them under birds – insects – reptiles – mammals.

Follow-up activities
▲ Make a simple graph of the children's different eye colours.
▲ Read *The owl who was afraid of the dark* by Jill Tomlinson (Mammoth).
▲ Learn about the work of the Guide Dogs for the Blind Association.

Keeping warm and dry

Objective
Design and Technology – to make a waterproof cloak for Red Riding Hood.

Group size
Small groups.

What you need
A collection of materials and fabrics (including cotton, nylon, plastic, foil, wool), sticky tape, string, scissors, a small doll, a plant sprayer and water, tissues.

What to do
Ask the children what Red Riding Hood would need to keep her warm and dry if it rained when she went to visit Granny.

Explain that they are going to make a pretty waterproof cloak for the doll, who represents Red Riding Hood. Let them choose different materials and make a cloak, fastening it around the doll when it's complete. Test the waterproof quality by spraying the cloak with the water spray.

Depending on their results the children could work to improve their designs. Dry the doll and re-test using the water spray.

Discussion
Ask what their own waterproof coats and macs are made from and talk about wet-weather clothing. Then ask if they can choose a waterproof material for their cloak. Say: we want to make a pretty cloak. Can you use more than one material to make it pretty and waterproof? Ask: how will it fasten? Can you make it stronger/warmer/dryer?

For younger children
Help them with cutting and fastening the cloaks.

For older children
Ask them to draw their ideas on paper before they make their cloaks.

Follow-up activities
▲ Make a collection of wet-weather gear.
▲ Keep a weather chart.
▲ Find out how umbrellas work.

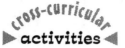

Little Red Riding Hood's cloak

Objective
History – to look at coats and cloaks through the ages.

Group size
Small groups or whole class.

What you need
A range of pictures of costumes of different periods – such as Roman, Medieval, Tudor, Georgian, Victorian and modern, a simple timeline.

Preparation
Make the timeline.

What to do
Explain that Red Riding Hood was wearing a cloak to keep her warm but that fashions have changed over the years and that warm clothing today looks different than it did in the past. Look at the pictures that you have of modern day clothing with the children and talk about the styles of clothing.

Display the timeline and place the modern-day outfit in the right place. Working back in time show the children the different period clothing in the pictures you have and place them on the right section of the timeline. Draw attention to similarities and differences.

Discussion
Ask the children what sort of clothes they wear today to keep warm. Encourage them to realise that clothing is designed to keep the heat in and cold winds out. Show the children the modern pictures and compare them as you show the older period dress. Say: how is this different to clothes you would wear? How is it the same as we wear? Would it keep you warm? Why? What do you think it is made from?

For younger children
Limit the number of time periods and examples you use.

For older children
Let them make a collection of wool and other fabrics which would have been used in different times.

Follow-up activities
▲ Have dressing-up clothes from different historical times.
▲ Make a collage of summer and winter clothes.
▲ Use the computer program *Teddy grids* on *My World 2* (Semerc).

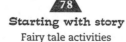

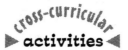
The path through the woods

Objective
Geography – to make a simple map.

Group size
Small groups.

What you need
One A2 sheet of paper, A4 sheets of paper, pencils, crayons or coloured pencils, felt-tipped pens.

What to do
Remind the children of Red Riding Hood's journey through the woods. Discuss the features of a wood which she might have seen. Tell the group that you are going to make a map of Red Riding Hood's walk through the forest.

Draw a pathway going round the A2 sheet and add trees, bridges, hills, rivers, rocks, the woodcutter's hut and other features. On the A4 sheets let the children draw their own pathways to show Red Riding Hood's route through the woods.

Discussion
Talk about the different things that Red Riding Hood might see as she walked through the forest. Ask: would all the trees look the same? Would the path be straight or with bends? How would she cross rivers and streams? Who might live in the woods? Would there be any buildings there?

For younger children
Give younger children some ideas of things to put in the woods before they draw their pathway.

For older children
Ask them to draw more than one path through the woods.

Follow-up activities
▲ Look at the different routes and paths around school.
▲ Go for a walk in the park, following a path.
▲ Play with playmats showing roads and paths through towns and villages.

Shades of red

Objective
Art – to explore colour mixing.

Group size
Small groups or whole class.

What you need
Red, black, white, blue and yellow paint, brushes, palettes, water pots, collection of different red artefacts and pictures, paper, sticky tape.

Preparation
Draw a grid on the paper as shown.

What to do
Tell the children that they are going to make Red Riding Hood's cloak in many shades of red. Look at the red artefacts and discuss all the shades of red available.

Demonstrate how to mix different shades of red paint by starting with pure red and adding small amounts of black. Paint a dab of this colour in the first box. Repeat the process gradually adding more black.

Invite the children to choose another colour to add to red and complete their grids in the same way. When all the grids are completed and dry, tape them together to make a patchwork cloak.

Discussion
Ask: what happens when we add a little more black? Is it darker or lighter? How does it alter the colour? When the children add their own colours say, what has happened to the red now? How has it changed? Can you think of anything that is the same colour red as this? When the grids are completed, count the coloured boxes together.

For younger children
Limit the number of boxes on the grid.

For older children
Help them to make up names for the shades of red they have invented. (Show them a paint colour chart).

Follow-up activities
▲ Make a 'red' corner collection.
▲ Learn about traffic lights.
▲ Dye some fabric red.

Musical portraits

Objective
Music – to listen to music and compose simple story accompaniments.

Group size
Small groups or whole class.

What you need
A tape or recording of Prokofiev's 'Peter and the wolf', a selection of instruments, cassette recorder and blank cassette.

Preparation
Tape the 'wolf', 'duck' and 'Peter' sections of the music.

What to do
Tell the children they are going to compose some music to go with the story of Red Riding Hood. Explain that composers often write music to accompany or represent stories.

Play the recorded music, section by section, stopping after each 'character' to discuss the different sounds. Remind them of the story of Red Riding Hood and let the children choose instruments which they think are suitable to play for mother, Red Riding Hood, woodcutter, wolf and granny.

Let them decide how to play the instruments and practise their ideas. Retell the story bringing the children in to play at the right moment for their character. Rehearse and then run the cassette, repeating the story and recording the performance. Listen to the composition!

Discussion
When listening to 'Peter and the wolf' ask: is that good music for a boy/wolf/duck? Why? Ask them to say whether it is fast/slow, loud/soft, high/low. When the children choose instruments ask: which instrument would be good to play the wolf and how will you play it? Can you make up a little wolf tune? Encourage them to rehearse and improve it by saying: is that the best loudness/speed/rhythm? Ask them to demonstrate different ways of playing.

For younger children
Spread the activity over two sessions, listening and then composing.

For older children
Play the whole of 'Peter and the wolf' over several sessions.

Follow-up activities
▲ Listen to music from different cultures.
▲ Learn to sing, 'Who's afraid of the big, bad wolf?'
▲ Invite visitors in to demonstrate stringed, brass and woodwind instruments.

Wolf's tail

Objective
PE – to use space appropriately and improve co-ordination.

Group size
Whole class.

What you need
A large space, a band or long ribbon for each child, a tambourine (or similar).

Preparation
Ask the children to change into pumps/bare feet and appropriate clothing.

What to do
Explain that the wolf was very good at escaping from hunters, running quickly through the forest with his tail flying out behind him. Now say they are going to play at 'Wolf's tail'.

Let each child tuck the band into the top of their shorts behind them. In pairs, one child chases the other to pull out the 'tail'. When caught they swap over. Remind the children not to be too violent in removing the 'tail'!

Next ask two children to be wolf and woodcutter. Everyone else sits or stands to make forest trees. The pair chase, dodging around the obstacles. When you sound the tambourine, the children swap roles. Repeat several times. Give the children turns or have several pairs working at once.

Discussion
Stop the children and ask: did you run in a straight line or dodge about? Which movement made it harder to catch you? Why? Encourage body swerving movements and use children to demonstrate saying: can you tell me when s/he dodges well?

For younger children
Use long bands and use the tambourine to swap over roles in the first tag activity.

For older children
Let several chasers collect 'tails' and see who can collect the most. Children who are caught 'freeze' to make trees.

Follow-up activities
▲ Play relay team games passing a band.
▲ Play 'hunt the tail', hiding a band in the room.
▲ Find out about wolves living in packs.

Caring for granny

Objective
RE – to think about the needs of the elderly and how people can help.

Group size
Small group or whole class.

What you need
Pictures of old people, sugar paper, felt-tipped pens, paper, pencils, crayons or colouring pencils, scissors, glue and spreaders.

Preparation
Fold the sugar paper to make a large book and title it, 'How we can help old people'.

What to do
Show the children the pictures of old people and explain that Red Riding Hood was going to visit her elderly granny to care for her. Ask the children about old people they know or have seen, and discuss the changes that happen to our bodies as we grow old.

Make a group list of the things children could do to help old people. When you have a suitable selection write one idea on each page of the book. Encourage the children to draw pictures to show each idea, cut them out and stick them on to the appropriate pages of the book to illustrate the suggestions.

Discussion
Ask why old people may find it more difficult to move around easily or carry heavy shopping. Explain how a fall can be dangerous for them. Ask, can you run around easily? If you fall over, do you often break bones? What might make an old person fall over? Say: what can grown-ups do to help? What can children do? Encourage children to talk about their own experiences with their families and friends, being sensitive to individual family circumstances. Talk about their pictures and ideas and ask them to choose which page their work will go on.

For younger children
Suggest ways that adults help the elderly and ways they could help too.

For older children
Let them write their own words and sentences to go with their illustrations.

Follow-up activities
▲ Make a collection of items for 'Help the aged'.
▲ Invite an old person in to talk about changes in their lives
▲ Make a greetings card for grandparents or an old people's home.

Through the woods

Group size
Small groups.

What you need
Small sticks, foam scraps, brown, green and yellow paints, small trays (to hold paints), backing paper, some leaves, paper, scissors, glue and spreaders, card, felt-tipped pens, fabric scraps.

Preparation
Using the card, make templates of the characters of the story. Put backing paper up in the display area.

What to do
Tell the children they are going to make a display of the woods and Red Riding Hood's journey to Granny's house, hiding all the main characters in the trees for people to find. Demonstrate how to use the length of the sticks to create trunks and branches by dipping them in the paint and printing with them. Then look at the leaves and use a variety of foam scraps to add prints of the leaf shapes, mixing greens, browns and yellows to get a good effect.

Ask the children to draw round the character templates and cut them out.

Colour them in and use fabric scraps to decorate them. Let the children decide where they will go.

Paint a pathway around the trees. Cut out the remaining trees from paper, paint them and stick them on so that the figures are peeping round them. Add the title: 'Who can you find in the woods?' and ask older children to add labels saying where the figures are, such as 'Granny is beside the biggest tree, Wolf is behind this tree'.

Discussion
Ask the children to look out of the windows and tell you about the shape of trees and the different colours and shapes of leaves. Discuss how the colours change when other paints are added. Ask: would the leaves look the same in spring, summer, and autumn? What would the trees look like in winter? Use positional language to help them to describe where they want the figures to be – asking, in front of the tree or behind it?

Follow-up activities
▲ Look at different trees and shrubs.
▲ Collect leaves and berries and identify them using a reference book.

Prints made from sticks and leaves

cut out trees

'The woodcutter is behind the tree.

Granny is on the path

Who can you find in the woods? Where are they hiding?

painted path

Inside Granny's cottage

Inside Granny's Cottage

Patchwork cloak in shades of red

Bathroom

Bedroom

Four shoe-boxes pinned to display board

Kitchen

Sitting room

Granny's favourite chair

furniture made from reclaimed materials

What else does Granny need?

Group size
Small groups.

What you need
Backing paper, several sheets of A2 paper, the red colour grids from page 80 'Shades of red' or similar, four similar sized cardboard boxes (for example shoe boxes), paper, matchboxes, cotton reels, LEGO, scraps of wood, foil, fabric and other small reclaimed materials, glue, spreaders, scissors, paint, felt-tipped pens and colouring pencils, sticky tape.

Preparation
Ask a small child to lie down on a large sheet of paper and draw around their outline to use as a template for creating the back view of Red Riding Hood. Stick the colour grids (from page 80) together like a patchwork to make her hood and cloak and fasten them securely. Fix the 'cloak' to the figure template and stick the figure on the display area.

What to do
Tell the children that they are going to make the rooms in Granny's cottage for the display. Talk about the things she might have in her home. Show each group one box and decide which room they will make. Use the various materials to decorate and furnish the rooms. When the rooms are completed, fix them together and add to the display (pin through the box in several places). Add the title, 'Inside Granny's cottage'. Let the children use small LEGO and Plasticine to make furniture. Ask older children to add a label to their furniture such as: 'Granny's favourite chair'.

Discussion
Talk about upstairs and downstairs in houses, bungalows and flats and stress the differences and similarities. Discuss the different things that decorate them (wallpaper, paint, pictures, posters, mirrors, ornaments and photographs) and the furniture. Ask them to look at the various materials and choose things which will help them make the different objects. Ask: is this about the right size? Where will it go?

Follow-up activities
▲ Look at different types of homes – flats, bungalows and houses.
▲ Count the windows/doors in your room.
▲ Find out about animals' homes.

Red Riding Hood's picnic

Group size
Small groups.

What you need
Small brown and white rolls, spread, a range of fillings (make sure no children are allergic to any of these), fruit, crisps, cake, biscuits, knives, spoons, plates, foil and sandwich bags, a basket, small tablecloth, paper serviettes.

What to do
Explain that Red Riding Hood had made up a picnic basket of food to take to her granny. Show the children the basket and cloth and tell them they are going to make up a picnic to share. Ask them to wash their hands.

Demonstrate spreading the rolls and filling them and then let the children choose fillings and prepare their own. Cut the cake and fruit into sufficient portions for each child. Show them how to wrap the foodstuffs in foil and bags. Put all the items in the basket and go for a walk, find a good spot to spread the cloth and share the picnic.

Afterwards, older children could try to write out instructions for preparing the picnic and draw pictures in sequence to show the activity.

Discussion
Ask: how many rolls will we need to have one each? Count them together. Ask: which filling will you choose? Why do you like it? Is it sweet or savoury? As you cut the fruit and cake, talk about halves and quarters and count and match the portions. Ask: how many biscuits do we need so that everyone gets two? Will we have enough cake? How many more slices do we need?

Follow-up activities
▲ Make cakes and sweets for a group party or to sell at a stall at a Christmas or summer Fair.
▲ Try making fruit squash and share it with the class.
▲ Make a simple salad lunch and invite a visitor to share it.

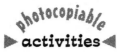

photocopiable
► activities ◄

What comes next?

Starting with story
Fairy tale activities

photocopiable
▶ **activities** ◀

Build a castle

▲ Build a castle from the shapes.

▲ Cut out and colour.

Make a dwarf

▲ 89
Starting with story
Fairy tale activities

The seven dwarfs

Old and new

▲Colour the old things Sleeping Beauty would have used in blue.

▲Colour the new things we would use now in red.

Sheep's wool

▲ Trace and cut out of card.

Cinderella's day (P59)
Dressed for the ball! (P64)

photocopiable
▶ **activities** ◀

Dressed for the ball!

▲ Dress the figure for the ball

To the palace

▲How does Cinderella get to the palace?

Visiting Granny

Starting with story
Fairy tale activities

Story puppets (P73)
What big eyes you have! (P76)

photocopiable
▶ **activities** ◀

Match the eyes

▲Join the eyes to the correct human or animal